Rand McNally

Children's
World
Atlas

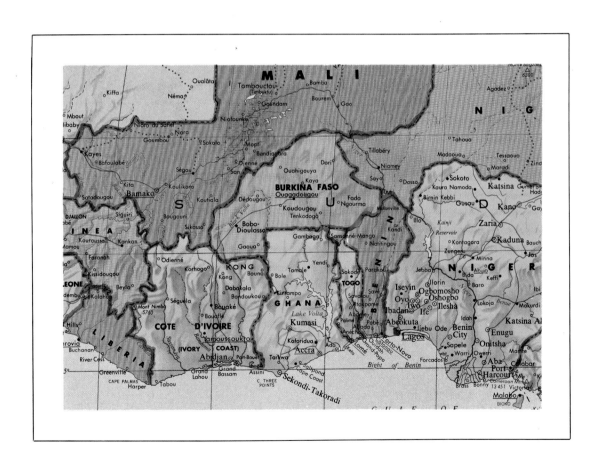

Rand McNally

Chicago • New York • San Francisco

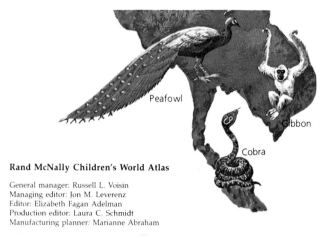

Peafowl

Gibbon

Cobra

Rand McNally Children's World Atlas

General manager: Russell L. Voisin
Managing editor: Jon M. Leverenz
Editor: Elizabeth Fagan Adelman
Production editor: Laura C. Schmidt
Manufacturing planner: Marianne Abraham

Rand McNally Children's World Atlas
Copyright © 1994 by Rand McNally & Company
Revised Printing, 1995

Photograph Credits
Pages 6-7: Pakistan/Ric Ergenbright; Alps/Rand McNally Pictorial World Atlas. **22-23:** Alps/Rand McNally Pictorial World Atlas; County Kerry/Ric Ergenbright; Mikonos/Rand McNally Student's World Atlas. **29:** Eiffel Tower/Joe Viesti. **34:** China and Pakistan/Ric Ergenbright. **40 and cover:** Jerusalem/Rand McNally Pictorial World Atlas, Colour Library International Limited. **44-45:** Zambia/Rand McNally Atlas of Mankind; Gulf of Guinea/Anna Tully, Hutchinson Picture Library. **50 and cover:** Masai/Rand McNally Children's World Atlas; **51:** Tunisia/R.G. Williamson, Telegraph Colour Library; Zimbabwe/Christopher Arnesen, Allstock. **56-57:** Australia/Robert Ivey, Ric Ergenbright Photography; New Caledonia/ Christopher Arnesen, Allstock. **64-65:** Caribbean/Nathan Benn, Allstock; Monument Valley and British Columbia/Ric Ergenbright. **70-71 and cover:** Mexico City/Rand McNally Pictorial World Atlas; Washington D.C./Art Wolfe, Allstock. **78-79:** Peru/Ric Ergenbright; Guyana/Hutchinson Picture Library; Paraguay/Peter Keen, Telegraph Colour Library. **84-85:** Suriname/R. Phillips, Image Bank; Rio de Janerio/Robert Ivey, Ric Ergenbright Photography; Ecuador/Rand McNally Pictorial World Atlas. **89:** Antarctica/Rand McNally Pictorial World Atlas.

Every effort has been made to trace the copyright holders of the photographs in this publication. Rand McNally apologizes in advance for any unintentional omissions and would be pleased to insert the appropriate acknowledgment in any subsequent edition of this book.

Library of Congress Cataloging-in-Publication Data

Rand McNally and Company.
 Rand McNally children's world atlas. -- Rev. ed.
  p. cm.
 Rev. ed. of: Rand McNally children's atlas of
the world. 1992.
 Includes index.
 Summary: Presents maps showing
world's terrain, climate, major economic
activities and populations.
 ISBN 0-528-83455-X
 1. Children's atlases. [1. Atlases.]
I. Rand McNally and Company.
Rand McNally children's atlas of the
world. II. Title. III. Title: Children's
world atlas.
G1021.R28 1992b < G&M >
912--dc20   92-39525
                                    CIP
                                 MAP AC

Contents

Our Planet Earth
A World of Terrain

Types of Terrain

	Ice and Snow
	Grassland
	Broadleaf Trees
	Tundra and Alpine
	Desert
	Needleleaf Trees
	High Barren Area
	Dry Scrub
	Tropical Rainforest

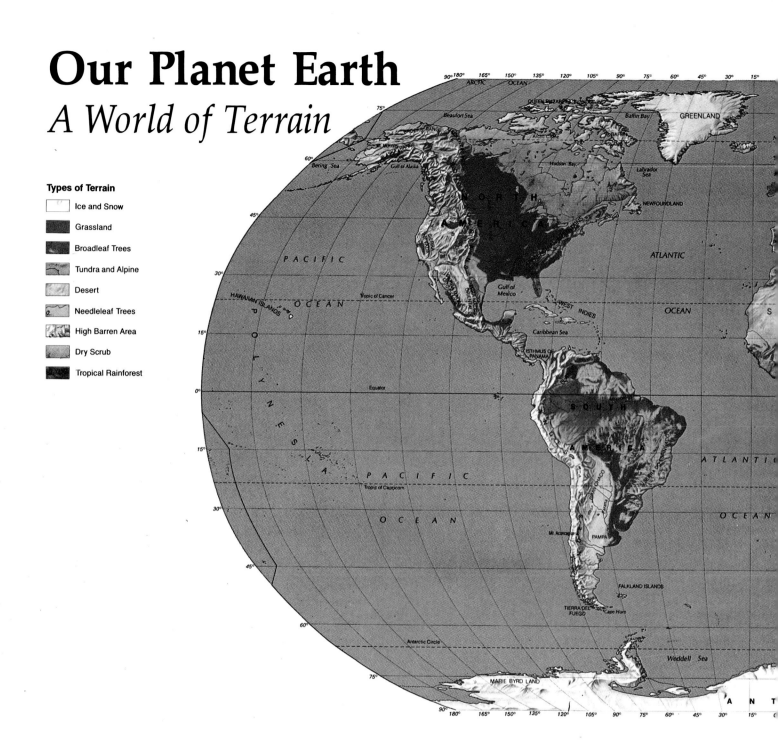

This map shows the world's *terrain*, or the different types of land that can be found on the surface of the earth. The colors and shading of the areas on the map indicate the kind of terrain found in that area of the world. The *legend* to the left of the map explains what the colors mean.

The earth's surface is a wrinkled layer of solid rock called the *crust*, which constantly changes. The crust is cracked into a dozen separate fragments called *tectonic plates*, which float on a sea of dense, semi-liquid rock far below. Columns of this molten rock slowly rise and fall within the earth, nudging the bases of the crustal plates that float on the surface. As the plates try to move, they push into their neighbors.

Sometimes two plates may lock together as they grind past one another. Pressure builds in the rock over many years; then suddenly the rock shatters and the plates slip. This movement creates earthquakes. Volcanoes rumble to

life when molten rock from the interior of the earth finds its way to the surface.

Over millions of years, the pushing and grinding of tectonic plates has crumpled, folded, and lifted rock, slowly building up the world's great mountain ranges in million-year-long collisions between the continents. For instance,

the Appalachian Mountains that run along North America's eastern coast are the result of a collision with Africa that occurred some 320 million years ago. Likewise, the Himalayas, the highest mountains of the world, were forced upward when India rammed into Asia. On this map, you can easily see where the

earth's mountains are.

The map also clearly shows the world's desert regions. Deserts are dry lands with low rainfall and sparse plant and animal life. Not all deserts are hot, sandy, and sunny. They can also be cold, rocky, or ice covered.

A World of Climate

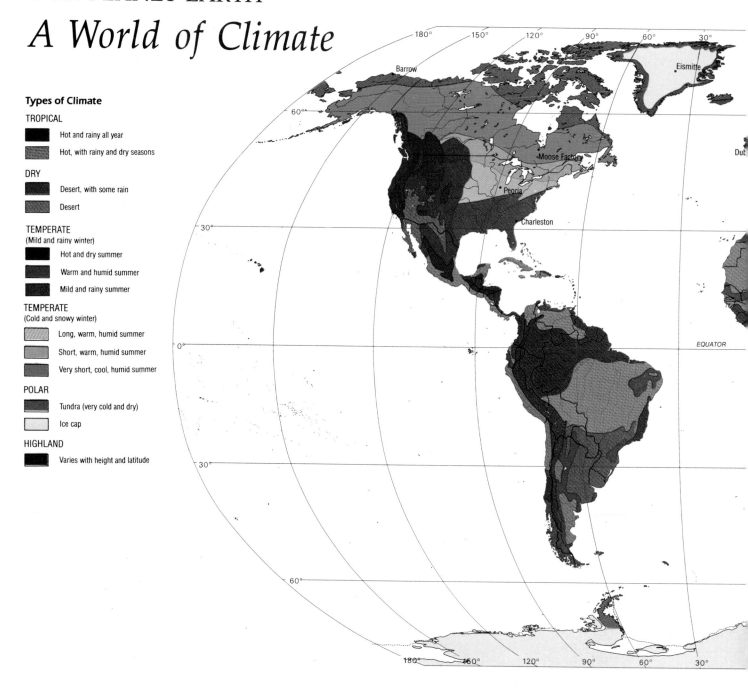

Types of Climate

TROPICAL
- Hot and rainy all year
- Hot, with rainy and dry seasons

DRY
- Desert, with some rain
- Desert

TEMPERATE
(Mild and rainy winter)
- Hot and dry summer
- Warm and humid summer
- Mild and rainy summer

TEMPERATE
(Cold and snowy winter)
- Long, warm, humid summer
- Short, warm, humid summer
- Very short, cool, humid summer

POLAR
- Tundra (very cold and dry)
- Ice cap

HIGHLAND
- Varies with height and latitude

This map shows the climates of the world. The colors of the different areas on the map tell you the kind of climate found in that area of the world. The legend to the left of the map will help you match the map's colors to the type of climate.

Climate and weather are not the same thing. *Weather* describes the temperature and *precipitation*—rain, snow, or other moisture—of an area during a short time. Climate, on the other hand, describes the same things but for a much longer period of time. It takes many years to determine a region's climate.

The climate we live in directly affects our lifestyles.

From the types of clothing we wear to the kind of food we eat, from the way we travel from one place to another to the kinds of homes we live in—all are dictated by climate.

Climates around the world vary for different reasons. In general, the world's climates are hotter closer to the equator and get colder as you go far-

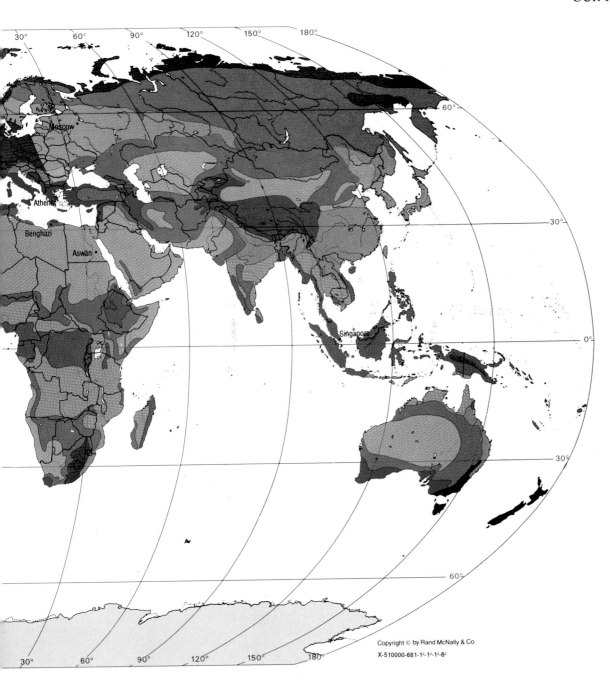

Copyright © by Rand McNally & Co.
X-510000-681-1ʲ-1ʲ-1ʲ-6ʲ

ther north or south. In addition, climates can be affected by large bodies of water, ocean currents, and by the terrain.

Water evaporates from the oceans, rises, cools, forms droplets, and falls as rain onto the land. Usually, the heaviest areas of precipitation in the world are along the equator,

where warm, tropical air can hold the greatest amount of water vapor. The reddish areas on the map show the world's tropical climates—the great rain forests of South America, central Africa, and Indonesia lie here, straddling the equator.

Terrain can have a major effect on precipitation. When the

terrain assists the rise of moist air, the pattern of rainfall can change dramatically. Mountain ranges force moist air to rise over them, often creating heavy rains on one side of the range and very little on the other. Moist air raised by mountains affects the rainfall in southern Alaska, western Norway, and southern Chile.

OUR PLANET EARTH
A World of Activity

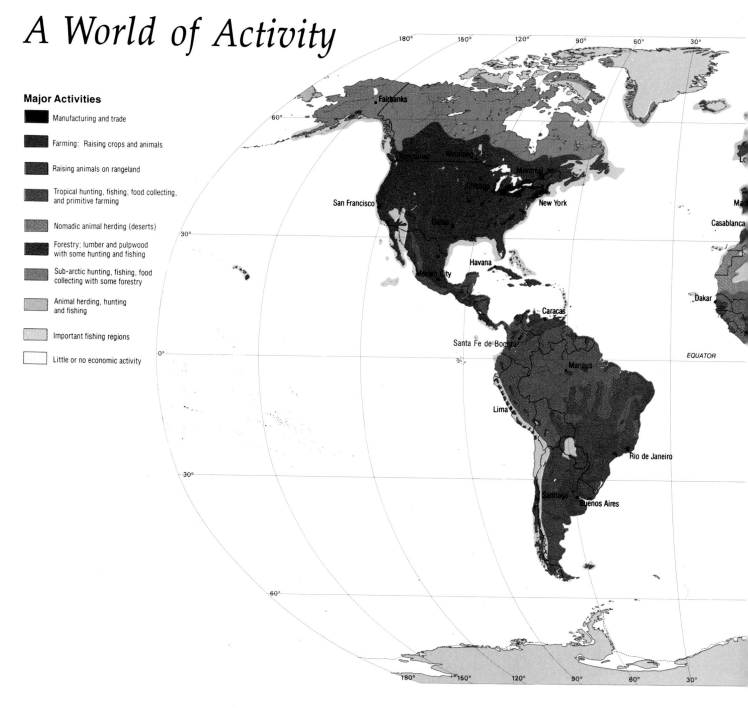

Major Activities

- Manufacturing and trade
- Farming: Raising crops and animals
- Raising animals on rangeland
- Tropical hunting, fishing, food collecting, and primitive farming
- Nomadic animal herding (deserts)
- Forestry; lumber and pulpwood with some hunting and fishing
- Sub-arctic hunting, fishing, food collecting with some forestry
- Animal herding, hunting and fishing
- Important fishing regions
- Little or no economic activity

This map shows the major economic activities of the world. The colors of the different areas on the map tell you what most of the people do for a living in that area of the world. Use the legend as you look at the map.

The character of the land has much to do with its use. In general, the farmed areas shown on the map are among the most fertile on earth. The fertile plains of Europe, southeastern Asia, and central North America feed much of the world's billions. Agriculture occupies most of the working population of India and China. In Brazil and the nations of eastern Europe, a much smaller part of the work force raises crops. And this fraction is smaller still in Canada, the United States, and western Europe.

You can see that very few regions of the world are used for manufacturing and trade. These areas are sometimes called *developed*, and they became developed for a variety of reasons. In the United

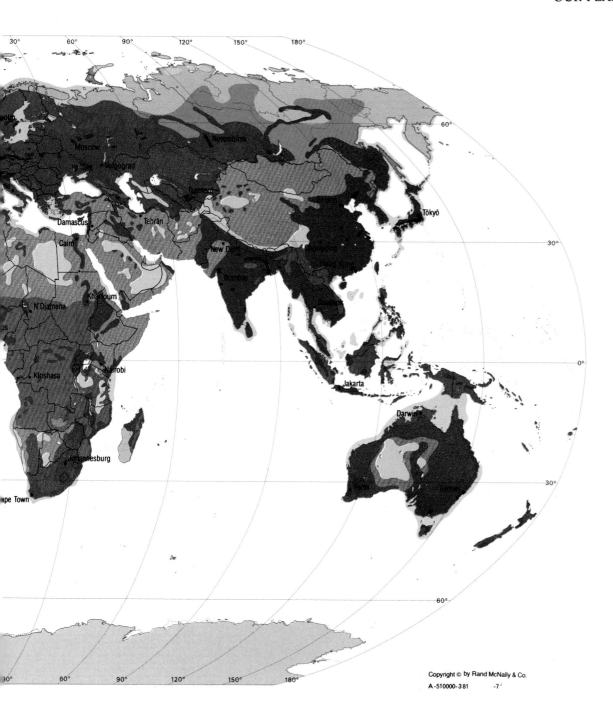

States, for instance, many developed areas grew up near natural resources and transportation routes. Major manufacturing centers such as Chicago and Montreal line the shores of the Great Lakes and the St. Lawrence seaway, an important transportation route that provides access to the Atlantic Ocean. Germany has become a major force in European industry. And tiny Japan, smaller than the U.S. state of California, leads Asia with its manufacturing might.

Compare this map to the terrain map. You can often tell what the people in an area of the world do by knowing what the land is like. For example, there is usually a lot of fishing along coastlines. Some of the world's most productive fishing areas include the coasts of North America, Europe, and the eastern coast of Asia. But sometimes you cannot predict what people do by the land on which they live. For example, people may live on good farmland, but they may not be able to farm it efficiently.

A World of People

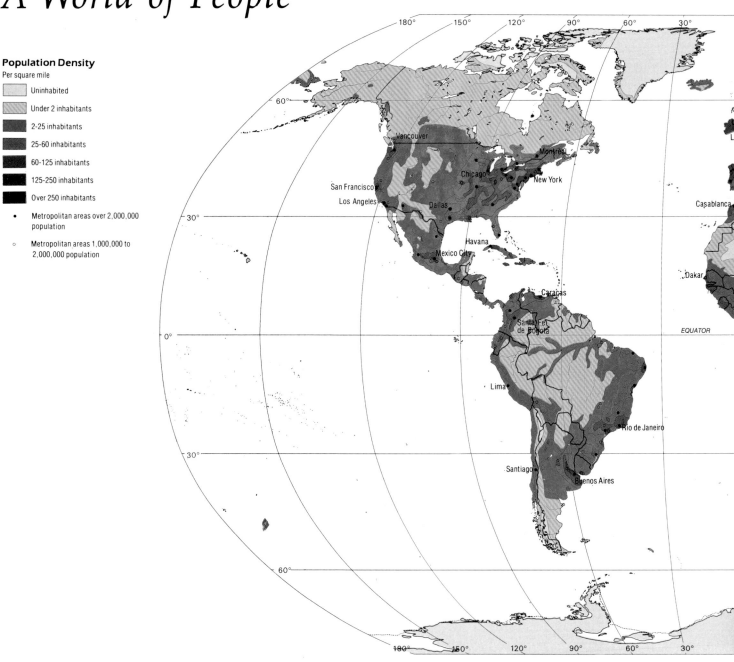

Population Density
Per square mile

- Uninhabited
- Under 2 inhabitants
- 2-25 inhabitants
- 25-60 inhabitants
- 60-125 inhabitants
- 125-250 inhabitants
- Over 250 inhabitants

- ● Metropolitan areas over 2,000,000 population
- ○ Metropolitan areas 1,000,000 to 2,000,000 population

This map shows where people live. Different colors tell you how many people are found in that area of the world. The legend tells you what the colors mean in terms of *population density*. This is a measure of the number of people living in each square mile (2.59 square kilometers) of land.

Naturally, population densities vary for many reasons, including climate and terrain. For example, the continent of Antarctica—the coldest region on Earth—is *uninhabited*, meaning that no one lives there permanently. The harsh climate makes settlement nearly impossible.

Lands with favorable climates and terrains tend to be densely populated, especially if they are good for farming. The ribbon of dense population that runs north through the desert lands of Sudan and Egypt is explained by the Nile River. The people here stay close to its fertile shores. In South America, in the vast rain forest, people settle along

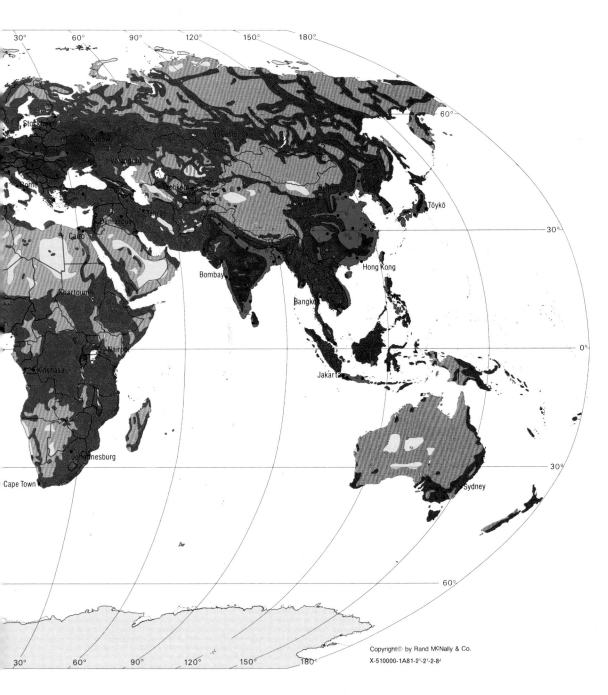

the Amazon River.

Look for the red and purple regions—the world's most thickly populated areas. The huge populations of India and China mostly live in the regions' rich farmlands. In such countries as China, India, and Turkey most of the people still live in country, or *rural*, areas away from cities.

In Europe and the United States, the most populous areas— the cities, or *urban* areas—grew up near farmland, resources, and trade routes, especially waterways. In the United States, the population is concentrated along the northeastern coast, the shores of the Great Lakes, and the banks of the Mississippi,

and along the West Coast. Cities hold the greatest part of the population of Australia, Argentina, Canada, France, Japan, and the United States.

One of the world's most densely populated nations is Japan. This country is slightly smaller than the state of California but holds a population of over 124 million people.

A World of Nations

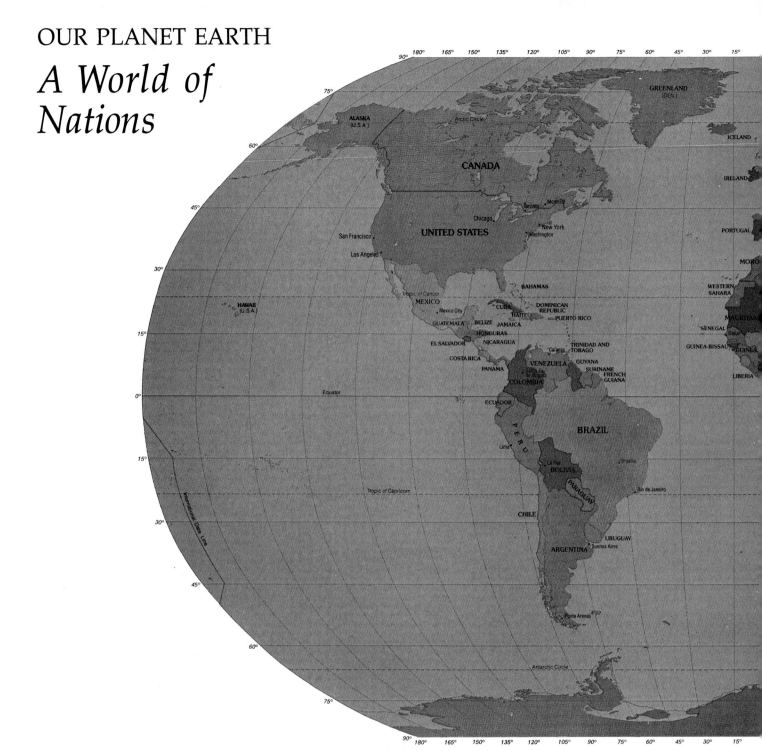

T his map shows the countries of the earth. The colors simply make it easier to see each separate country on the map; they do not tell you anything about each nation. This type of map is called *political* because it shows the world's political divisions.

National borders are represented on the map as thin red lines. These lines divide the world into separate countries. Sometimes they follow natural formations such as mountain ranges or rivers. For example, the crooked northwestern border of China runs along a river. In some cases, though, the line is designated by humans—as with the straight portion of the border between Canada and the United States.

Although most political borders in today's world are well established, changes still occur. In 1990, for instance, East and West Germany united, and Germany became a single nation. In 1991, the Soviet Union dissolved, and many nations that had been a part of the union became independent.

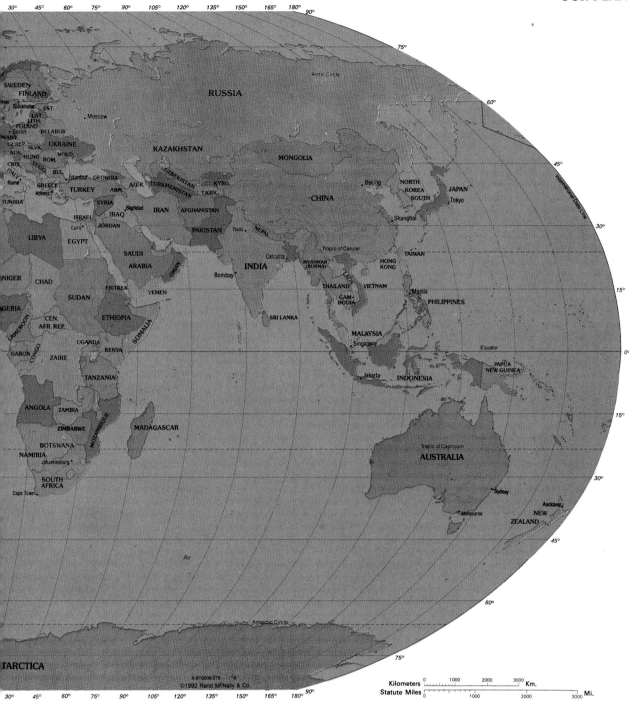

Some countries are large, and some countries are small. Russia and Canada are huge nations. The world's smallest independent state is Vatican City, in Rome, Italy.

When people study the world, they often organize all the countries by land areas called *continents*. The seven continents are the great divi-sions of the earth. Nearly all of them are large pieces of land that are almost complete-ly surrounded by water.

This atlas divides the world into the seven continents: Eu-rope, Asia, Africa, North America, South America, Ant-arctica, and the area in the South Pacific called Oceania. The islands of the South Pacif-ic are grouped with Australia to form Oceania, but they are not actually part of Australia.

For each continent except Antarctica, there is a section on its *terrain*, or land areas; a discussion of its wild animals; a section about what the peo-ple who live there do for a liv-ing; and an overview of its countries and cities.

Using the Atlas

An atlas is a guide to the world that can be used in many ways. But to discover the world with your atlas, you must be able to do five things:

- Measure distances using a map scale.
- Use directions and latitude and longitude.
- Find places on the maps using map keys.
- Use different kinds of maps.
- Use map symbols and legends.

The following sections can help you learn how to do these things.

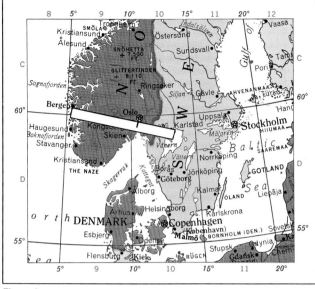

Figure 1

Measuring Distances

To understand a map, you must know its *scale*, or how large an area of the earth it shows. There are different types of map scales, but the *bar scale* is the easiest to use for finding distance.

For example, to find the distance between Bergen and Oslo in Norway, first you will find out how far Bergen is from Oslo on the map. Then, by using a bar scale, you will learn what this means in actual distance on the earth.

1. Find Bergen and Oslo on the map in Figure 1.
2. Lay a slip of paper on the map so its edge touches the two cities. Move the paper so one corner touches Bergen.
3. Mark the paper where it touches Oslo. The distance from the corner of the paper to the mark shows how far Oslo is from Bergen on the map.
4. The numbers in the map scale in Figure 2 show *statute miles*, or miles on

the earth. Line up the edge of the paper along the map scale, putting the corner at 0.
5. Find the mark on the paper. The mark shows that Bergen is about two hundred miles away from Oslo.

Using Directions and Latitude and Longitude

Most of the maps in this atlas are drawn so north is at the top of the page, south is at the bottom, west is at the left, and east is at the right.

Many of the maps also have lines drawn across them—lines of *latitude* and *longitude*. These are lines drawn on a map or globe to make it easier to tell directions and to locate places.

Latitude lines are also called *parallels*. As shown in Figure 3, lines of latitude run east and west. The equator is a line of latitude, and it runs around the middle of the earth. Other lines of latitude measure how far north or south of the equator a place is. Lines of latitude are numbered in *degrees*,

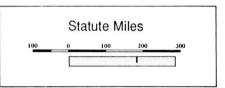

Figure 2

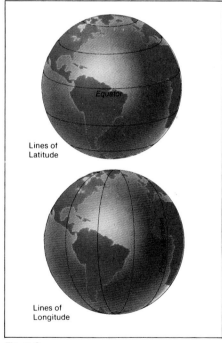

Figure 3

which measure the distance.

The equator is at zero degrees (0°) latitude. The numbers go up in each direction (north and south) the farther you get from the equator. The map in Figure 1 shows that Bergen is north of sixty degrees (60°) latitude and

Stockholm is south of it. So Bergen is farther north than Stockholm.

Lines of longitude run north and south between the two poles, as you can see from Figure 3. Longitude lines are also called *meridians*. Like latitude, longitude is also measured in degrees.

The *prime meridian* is at zero degrees (0°) longitude. Lines of longitude measure how far east or west a place is from the prime meridian. The numbers go up as you travel in each direction (east and west). In Figure 1, Bergen is about five degrees (5°) east of the prime meridian, and Stockholm is about twenty degrees (20°) east. So Stockholm is farther east than Bergen.

Using Map Keys

One of the most important things an atlas can do is tell you the location of a place. To help you find a place quickly and easily on a map, most atlases have an index that includes both the names of places and a guide that is made up of a letter and a number, or a *map key*.

Say you want to find Santiago, a city in Chile, which is in South America. Here's how you would use the map key.
1. Look up the city's name, Santiago, in the back of the atlas. You'll see an entry

Figure 4

like the one in Figure 4. The number *88* is the page on which the map is found. The map key *C2* is the letter-number guide to finding Santiago on the map on page 88.
2. Look at Figure 5. It is a piece of the map of southern South America that you will find on page 88.
3. Find the letters *A* through *C* along the left-hand side of the map. Then find the numbers *2* through *4* along the top edge of the map. These numbers and letters are centered between the lines of latitude and longitude on the map.
4. To find Santiago, use the map key *C2*. Place your left index finger on *C* and your right index finger on *2*. Move your left finger

across the map and your right finger down the map, staying within the

Figure 5

88 South America, South • Physical — Political

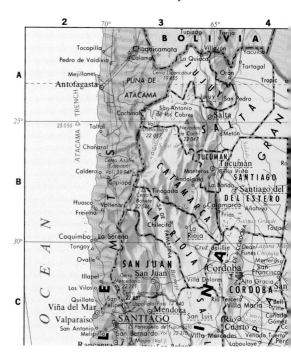

Parallels of latitude are always seventy miles apart. But the distance between meridians shrinks as they approach the North and South poles. At the equator, a giraffe must run seventy miles (112.65 kilometers) to cover one degree of longitude. Near the South Pole, a penguin could easily waddle one degree.

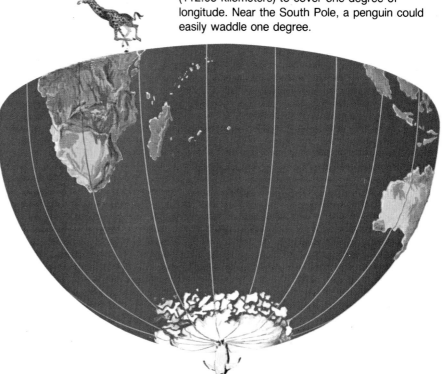

latitude and longitude lines on either side. Your fingers will meet in the box that contains Santiago.

You can use this method to find any place listed in the index of this atlas. If you see a small, or lowercase, letter in a map key, it refers to the small inset map on the page rather than to the main map on the page. Two map keys are shown for areas that begin on one map and continue on another map.

Using Different Kinds of Maps

There are many different types of maps, and each is especially suited for a certain purpose. For exploring the world's surface, *terrain maps* reveal rugged mountains and continental plains. For special subjects, such as the wildlife of a region, *thematic* maps provide an easy way to see differences throughout the world. For studying countries, *political maps* display the world's nations and cities, roads, and railways. The *physical-political* maps in this atlas tell you the most about each continent. They are the large maps on the pages all by themselves.

The terrain maps go along with the section on the terrain of each continent. These are also called *physical maps* because they show only the physical features of the land. Physical features include oceans, lakes, rivers, glaciers, mountains, and other natural parts of the world.

The thematic maps go with the sections on animals and life on the land. The thematic maps show pictures that tell you about different regions on the map. On the thematic map of the animals of North America, you can see that raccoons live around the Great Lakes. Similar maps throughout the atlas show the kinds of

Terrain Map

Thematic Map

Political Map

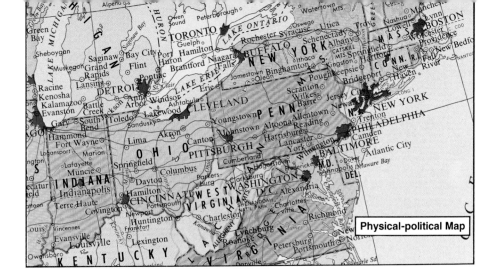

Physical-political Map

wildlife found on each continent. Another type of thematic map shows how people use the land of each continent.

The political maps show the world's political units, the human-made divisions of the earth's surface into countries, states, and cities. These maps go with the sections about countries and cities. They show you the boundaries of each country on the continent as well as the major cities. On the political map of North America, for instance, thick gray lines represent the boundaries of countries. Thinner gray lines show the borders between states or provinces. The thinnest gray lines reveal the locations of railroad tracks; red lines show the major roadways. Other countries, such as Canada and Mexico, are shaded with different colors.

When people think about maps, they usually picture physical-political maps. To get the most information out of these maps, you need to understand what the special symbols on each map represent. You can do that with the help of a *legend*, which is discussed in the next section.

Using Map Symbols and Legends

The easiest way to describe a *symbol* is that it is something that stands for something else. In a way, a whole map is a symbol, because it represents the world or a part of it.

The world's features—such as cities, rivers, and lakes—are represented with symbols on maps. The legend tells you what these symbols mean. On the physical-political maps in this atlas, the symbol for a city might be a dot or a red shaded area, depending on how big the city is. Rivers are shown with blue lines, and railroads are indicated with red lines.

The physical-political map legend at the right divides the earth's geographic features into three major classes: cultural, land, and water features. Cultural features are human-made and include cities, railroads, dams, and political boundaries. Land features are mountain peaks, mountain passes, and *spot heights*. Spot heights tell you the elevation of certain places on a mountain. Water features include rivers, lakes, swamps, and glaciers. Refer to this when working with the physical-political maps.

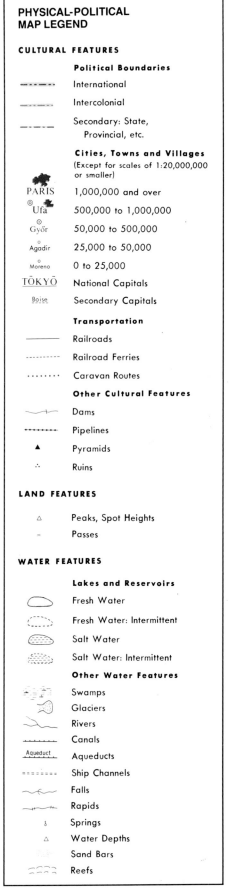

PHYSICAL-POLITICAL MAP LEGEND

CULTURAL FEATURES

Political Boundaries

-------	International
-------	Intercolonial
- - - -	Secondary: State, Provincial, etc.

Cities, Towns and Villages
(Except for scales of 1:20,000,000 or smaller)

PARIS	1,000,000 and over
◎ Ufa	500,000 to 1,000,000
◌ Győr	50,000 to 500,000
∘ Agadir	25,000 to 50,000
∘ Moreno	0 to 25,000
TŌKYŌ	National Capitals
Boise	Secondary Capitals

Transportation

———	Railroads
---------	Railroad Ferries
········	Caravan Routes

Other Cultural Features

⌒	Dams
·••••••••	Pipelines
▲	Pyramids
∴	Ruins

LAND FEATURES

△	Peaks, Spot Heights
=	Passes

WATER FEATURES

Lakes and Reservoirs

⬭	Fresh Water
⬭	Fresh Water: Intermittent
⬭	Salt Water
⬭	Salt Water: Intermittent

Other Water Features

	Swamps
	Glaciers
	Rivers
	Canals
Aqueduct	Aqueducts
========	Ship Channels
⌒	Falls
⌒	Rapids
ᵟ	Springs
△	Water Depths
	Sand Bars
⌒⌒⌒	Reefs

Europe

Sixth largest continent

•

Second in population: 712,100,000

•

32 cities with over 2 million population

•

Highest mountain: El'brus, 18,510 feet
(5,642 meters)

•

Rome and Chicago are the same
latitude

Europe
Terrain

Many parts of Europe lie under the shadows of towering mountains. The most splendid of these peaks are the Alps, which make up a mountain range that winds through Switzerland, southeastern France, Austria, southern Germany, northern Italy, and eastward into Slovenia. Three other mountain ranges spread out from the central mass of the Alps into other countries.

Across the English Channel from mainland Europe are the islands that form the United Kingdom. England lies on the biggest island, and central mountains called the Pennines run through that country like a bumpy backbone.

Northern mainland Europe

has many mountains. The uplands of Norway and Sweden are bleak and barren. Long ago huge rivers of ice called *glaciers* ground their way across this land, carving deep grooves in between the mountains. The grooves flooded with water from the sea and have become long waterways called *fjords*. Far to the east the Ural Mountains in Russia mark the division between Europe and Asia. To the southwest of the Alps, the Pyrenees separate France and Spain. Spain and Portugal lie on a *peninsula*, a body of land that is almost surrounded by water.

Many famous rivers flow from Europe's mountains. Perhaps the best known, the Rhine, flows north out of Switzerland, past France, and through Germany and the Netherlands. The Danube is another large river that flows through Germany.

The north-central part of Europe is a fertile area known as the Great European Plain. The rich farmlands of this region supply food for much of Europe, and its minerals help to make the Ruhr Valley on the Rhine River a world center for heavy industry.

Many islands lie to the south of mainland Europe in the Mediterranean Sea. They include Corsica, Sardinia, Sicily, and the isles of Greece. The warm, sunny beaches of the Mediterranean are popular with tourists.

County Kerry, in the southwest corner of Ireland, features green pastures and rugged coastlines.

The rugged, snow capped peaks of the Swiss Alps provide a splendid background for skiers. Tourism is an important part of Switzerland's economy.

Mykonos, shown here, and the other Greek islands in the Aegean Sea are part of the Pindus Mountains. Millions of years ago, a rising sea covered all but the mountain peaks.

EUROPE
Animals

Herring

Skua

Barnacle Goose

Reindeer

Grey Seal

Wolverine

Lemming

Hare

Basking Shark

Red Deer

Otter

Black Grouse

Badger

Pheasant

Hedgehog

Rabbit

Fox

Atlantic Salmon

Red-legged Partridge

Chamois

Moorhen

Marmot

Squirrel

Great Bustard

Stork

Barbary Ape

Sole

Ferruginous Duck

Hoopoe

Spanish Mackerel

Raven

Whimbrel

Brown Bear

Pine Marten

Wild Boar

Wolf

Griffon Vulture

Roe Deer

Lesser Spotted Eagle

Tur

Octopus

Conger Eel

Most of the vast, animal-filled forests that once covered much of Europe were cut down long ago to make room for farms, cities, and towns. Many of Europe's animals were hunted for centuries until they were wiped out. But in the few wild places that remain—mostly national parks and game preserves where animals are protected—some of the animals that once abounded in Europe can still be found.

Shaggy wild boars with curved tusks can be found in the forests of central Europe. Packs of wolves still live in some places, and in northern Russia, the huge brown bear still lumbers about.

Many smaller types of animals live in Europe. Foxes, badgers, moles, rabbits, and squirrels are found in many places. Plump little lemmings abound in the mountains of Norway and Sweden. The hedgehog is common in northern Europe.

Small, striped wildcats prowl in parts of eastern Europe. A rather large wildcat, the Spanish lynx, lives in Spain. Three feet (0.91 meter) long with pointed ears and thick whiskers, the lynx is a fast, fierce hunter.

Sparrows, thrushes, finches, nightingales, and ravens are found throughout central Europe. So are large birds of prey such as falcons and eagles. During the summer, the big white stork is a common sight in cities of the Netherlands, Belgium, and Germany, where it nests on the chimneys of houses.

In a protected forest of Poland about 1,600 *wisents*, bison of prehistoric Europe, feed in grassy clearings just as they did thousands of years ago. They stand up to six feet (1.82 meters) high at the shoulder.

EUROPE
Life on the Land

Fishing

Hydrothermal Plant

Reindeer Herding

Coal Mining

Lumbering

Agricultural Area

Fishing

Fishing

Canneries

Papermaking

Dairyland

Offshore Oil Drilling

Cheese Making

Dairyland

Troika
(3-horse Sleigh)

Agricultural

Agricultural Area

Heavy Industry

Farming

Houses of Parliament

Bulb Farming

Heavy Industry (Steel)

Dairyland

Grimm's Fairy Tale
Country

Eiffel Tower

Oil Fields

Vineyards

Citrus Groves

Export by Sea

Matterhorn

Wheatlands

Light
Industry

Sheep Raised

Cork Harvesting

Water Sports

Roman Ruins

Olive Orchards

Bullfighting

Opera

Vineyards

Vineyards

Ancient Greek Ruins

Fishing

The whole continent of Europe juts off of Asia and into the sea. No part of western Europe is more than three hundred miles from the sea. It is no wonder that many Europeans depend on fishing or sailing to make their living.

Between the many mountains of Europe lie most of Europe's farms. More than half of the land of Europe is used for farming. The raising of livestock is also important throughout Europe.

Modern industry, especially mining and manufacturing, began in Europe. Today, many world industrial leaders are European nations.

Europe's island nations, Iceland, Ireland, and Great Britain, are no less a part of the continent. The United Kingdom unites the four regions known as England, Scotland, Wales (together called Great Britain), and Northern Ireland. Climate limits agriculture, but the use of mechanized farming methods allows the nation to produce half its food supply.

The northern countries of Europe contain fewer people than the rest of the continent. The thick forests provide these countries with an important resource: wood. All three nations export pulp, paper, furniture, and other wood products.

Europe is smaller than any other continent except Australia. But it has more people than any other continent except for Asia. As a result, Europe is very densely populated.

EUROPE
Countries and Cities

Europe has seen many wars, most of them fought over pieces of land. Thus the boundaries of countries have shifted many times over the centuries. In the 1990s, East and West Germany reunited to again form a single Germany.

The republics that were part of the Soviet Union gained independence and Czechoslovakia divided to form the Czech Republic and Slovakia.

Usually, the borders of countries form around natural barriers, such as rivers, seas, or

mountain ranges. The reason for this is that these are places where people can easily defend themselves from attack. Many European nations are edged by such natural borders.

Today, most European countries elect their leaders. In

some countries, the descendants of the kings and queens that ruled most European countries in earlier times are still treated as royalty, but they do not rule the country.

Travelers to Europe must deal with the continent's many languages. Latin-speaking Romans once conquered much of Europe; today the French, Italians, Spanish, Portuguese, and Romanians speak different tongues—the so-called *Romance* languages—that are based on the ancient Latin. The people of Germany, the Netherlands, England, Denmark, Sweden, and Norway speak languages rooted in a single, ancient tongue—the German of the tribes that occupied those areas in ages past. To the east, the peoples of Poland, the Czech Republic, Slovakia, Bulgaria, and other eastern European nations speak languages based on Slavic dialects.

Europe has many big cities that are rich in history and culture. Rome, Italy, and Athens, Greece, were known thousands of years ago. Paris dates back more than two thousand years. It was founded around 52 B.C. by soldiers of the Roman Empire. Trondheim, in Norway, had its beginning around A.D. 998.

The city of Paris and its surrounding area make up the second largest metropolitan area in Europe. The Eiffel Tower, shown here, has become a symbol of French achievement.

© 1992 Rand McNally & Co.
X-550000-279

Roads
Railroads

40,000 SQ MI
AREA

0   100   200
Miles

Cities,
Towns,
and
Villages

0 to 25,000   ○   100,000 to 250,000   ⊙   1,000,000 and over   ◉

25,000 to 100,000   •   250,000 to 1,000,000   ◎   Major urbanized area

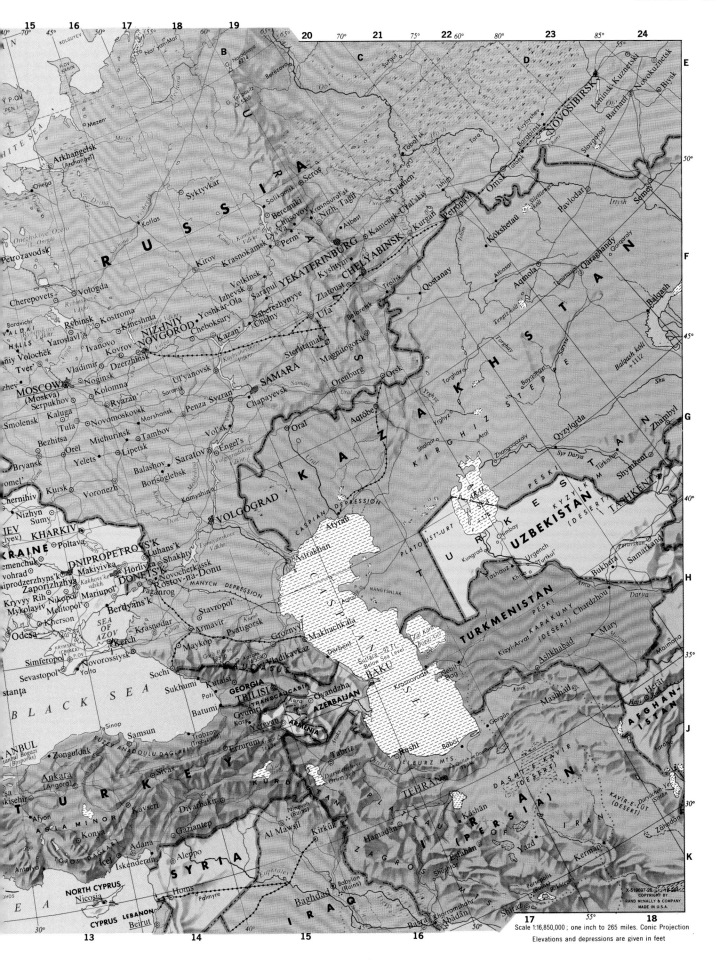

Scale 1:16,850,000 ; one inch to 265 miles. Conic Projection

Elevations and depressions are given in feet

ATLANTIC OCEAN

UNITED KINGDOM
Glasgow
Edinburgh
Aberdeen
Newcastle
NORTH SEA

NORWAY
SWEDEN
Bergen
Trondheim
Oslo
Göteborg
DENMARK
COPENHAGEN
Malmö
Kiel
HAMBURG
GERMANY
BERLIN
Poznań
POLAND
WARSAW
Łódź
Kraków
Ostrava

Gulf of Bothnia
FINLAND
Stockholm
Norrköping
Turku
Helsinki
BALTIC SEA
Gdańsk
Kaliningrad
LITHUANIA
Kaunas
Vilnius
Minsk
BELARUS
Brest
Baranovichi
Mogilëv

ESTONIA
Tallinn
Tartu
LATVIA
Riga
Vyborg
ST. PETERSBURG (Leningrad)
Pskov
Tikhvin
Velikiye Luki
Vitebsk

LAPLAND
Kiruna
Narvik
Murmansk
KOLA PEN.
WHITE SEA
Arkhangelsk (Archangel)
BARENTS SEA
NOVAYA ZEMLYA
KARSKOYE (Kara Sea)

UKRAINE
KIEV (Kiyev)
Lviv
Zhytomyr
Vinnytsya
Chernivtsi
MOLD.
Kishinëv
Odesa
Mykolayiv
Simferopol'
Sevastopol'
DNIPROPETROVS'K
Kryvyy Rih
Zaporizhzhya
KHARKIV
DONETS'K
Luhans'k

MOSCOW (Moskva)
Serpukhov
Smolensk
Bryansk
Orël
Kursk
Kaluga
Tula
Ryazan'
Lipetsk
Voronezh
Tambov
Penza
Saratov
NIZHNIY NOVGOROD
Vladimir
Murom
Saransk
Yaroslavl'
Ivanovo
Kostroma
Vologda
Cherepovets
Rybinsk
Tver'
Vyshniy Volochëk
Borovichi

Kirov
Perm
Izhevsk
Kazan'
Ufa
SAMARA
Ul'yanovsk
Syzran'
Buzuluk
Sterlitamak
Magnitogorsk
YEKATERINBURG
Nizhniy Tagil
Chelyabinsk
Kurgan
Tyumen'

WESTERN SIBERIAN LOWLAND
RUSSIA
Surgut
Khanty-Mansiysk
Omsk
NOVOSIBIRSK
Tomsk
Kemerovo
Barnaul
Rubtsovsk

KAZAKHSTAN
KIRGHIZ STEPPE
CASPIAN DEPRESSION
Atyrau
Astrakhan
Oral
Orenburg
Orsk
Aqtöbe
Qostanay
Petropavl
Aqmola
Pavlodar
Semey
Qaraghandy
Balqash
Zhezqazghan
Qyzylorda

CASPIAN SEA
Surface 92 feet below Sea Level
Makhachkala
Groznyy
CAUCASUS
GEORGIA
Tbilisi
ARMENIA
Yerevan
AZERBAIJAN
BAKU
Gyandzha
Krasnovodsk
ARAL SEA

BLACK SEA
Rostov-na-Donu
Volgograd
Stavropol'
Krasnodar
Novorossiysk
Sochi
Maykop
Armavir
Sea of Azov
Mariupol'

TURKEY
Samsun
Sinop
Trabzon
Erzurum
Malatya
Diyarbakir
KURDISTAN
IRAQ
Baghdad
Kirkūk
Al Mawsil

IRAN
TEHRAN
ELBURZ MTS.
Tabriz
Rasht
Zanjan
Hamadān
Mashhad
Ashkhabad
ZAGROS MTS.
GR. SALT DESERT
Eşfahān
Kāshān

TURKMENISTAN
PESKI KARAKUMY (DESERT)
UZBEKISTAN
TURKESTAN
PLATO UST'-URT
PESKI KYZYL KUM (DESERT)
Chardzhou
Bukhara
Samarkand
TASHKENT
TAJIK.
Dushanbe
KYRGYZSTAN
Bishkek
Alma-Ata (Almaty)
TIEN SHAN
CHINA
Ürümqi
Kashgar

Scale 1:21,500,000; one inch to 340 mi
Lambert's Azimuthal, Equal Area Projec
Elevations and depressions are given in

40,000 SQ. MI.
AREA

0   150   300
Miles

A   B   C   D   E   F

N

OCEAN

SEVERNAYA ZEMLYA
(NORTHERN LAND)

LAPTEV SEA

EAST SIBERIAN SEA

DE LONGA

NOVOSIBIRSKIYE OVA
(NEW SIBERIAN ISLANDS)

TAYMYR
GORY BYRRANGA
P.OV

GORY PUTORANA

S   I   B   E   R   I   A

YAKUT A.S.S.R.

KHREBET CHERSKOGO

VERKHOYANSKIY KHREBET

Yakutsk

KHREBET GYDAN (KOLYMSKIY)

KORYAKSKIY KHREBET

CHUKOTSKOYE NAGORYE

Arctic Circle

WRANGELYA (WRANGEL)

Magadan

KAMCHATKA

Petropavlovsk-Kamchatskiy

SEA OF OKHOTSK

SAKHALIN

DZHUGDZHUR KHREBET

STANOVOY KHREBET

PATOM PLATEAU

BURYAT A.S.S.R.

YABLONOVYY KHREBET

BAYKAL'SKIY KHREBET

Krasnoyarsk   Kansk   Tayshet
Bratsk
Nizhneudinsk   Tulun
Zhigalovo
Kachug
Barguzin
Cheremkhovo   Angarsk
Irkutsk   Ulan-Ude

TANNU-OLA

Kyzyl

MONGOLIA

Ulan Bator
(Ulaanbaatar)

HANGAYN NURUU
ARHANGAJ

GOBI OR SHAMO
(DESERT)

Hami

STANOVOY KHREBET

NERCHINSKIY KHREBET

Chita
Sretensk   Nerchinsk

Petrovsk-Zabaykal'skiy

Skovorodino

Svobodnyy
Belogorsk
Blagoveshchensk

KHREBET BUREINSKIY

Komsomol'sk-na-Amure

Sovetskaya Gavan'

SIKHOTE ALIN'

Nikolayevsk-na-Amure

Khabarovsk

USSURIYSK KHREBET

Birobidzhan

Harbin
Mudanjiang

Vladivostok
Nakhodka

Yuzhno-Sakhalinsk

HOKKAIDŌ
Sapporo
Otaru

GREATER KHINGAN RANGE
LESSER KHINGAN RANGE

MANCHURIA

Qiqihar

CHANGCHUN

Jilin

SHENYANG   FUSHUN

NORTH KOREA
P'yongyang

SOUTH KOREA
SEOUL

PUSAN

HONSHŪ

KYOTO
KOBE
OSAKA
Hiroshima

SEA OF JAPAN

C   H   I   N   A

Zhangjiakou

BEIJING   TIANJIN

Lüshun   Dalian

Baoding

YELLOW SEA

Bo Hai

Korea Bay

KOREA STRAIT

100 200 300 400 500 600 Miles
200 400 600 800 1000 Kilometers

Asia
Terrain

Asia

Largest continent

•

First in population: 3,422,700,000

•

57 cities with over 2 million population

•

World's highest mountain: Everest, 29,028 feet (8,848 meters)

•

World's largest "lake": Caspian Sea, 143,240 square miles (370,990 square kilometers)

•

World's lowest inland point: Dead Sea, 1,312 feet (400 meters) below sea level

Asia is the largest continent. It covers more area than North America, Europe, and Australia combined. Because it is so big, it is a land of many extremes. It has some of the world's highest mountains, longest rivers, largest deserts, and coldest and hottest climates.

Asia begins at the Ural Mountains in Russia and extends more than three thousand miles (almost five thousand kilometers), all the way to the Pacific Ocean. This northern region is known as Siberia.

To the south of Siberia is an equally large, equally harsh region. This area begins in the deserts of Saudi Arabia and sweeps across central Asia through Iraq, Iran, into Turkmenistan and Kazakhstan, through parts of China, and on into the deserts of Mongolia.

The region is bounded in the south by the highest mountains on the earth: the Himalayas. The mountains thrust up when the Indian subcontinent crashed into Asia millions of years ago. The two peaks that are considered the highest in the world, Mount Everest and K2, are in the Himalayas.

The erosion of limestone created this unusual cone-shaped hill near Guilin in southeastern China. Regions such as these are called *karst*. Images of karst can often be found in traditional Chinese art.

In northern Pakistan, apricots grown in the rugged terrain and harsh climate of the Himalayas dry in the sun. The highest mountains in the world, the Himalayas stretch some 1,550 miles (2,500 kilometers) across central Asia and cut across five countries.

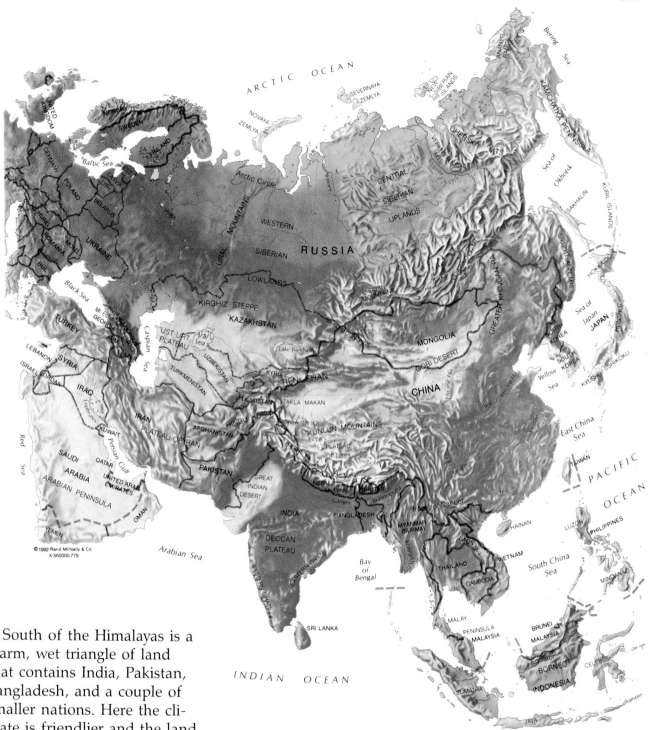

South of the Himalayas is a warm, wet triangle of land that contains India, Pakistan, Bangladesh, and a couple of smaller nations. Here the climate is friendlier and the land more fertile, so many people live in this area. In fact, this is one of the world's most crowded regions.

To the east lies Southeast Asia, a land that is a giant rain forest. It is very fertile and has plenty of rainfall. These factors make Southeast Asia a good place to live, so the countries of this region are highly populated.

North of Southeast Asia is an area known as the Far East. It includes most of China, North Korea, South Korea, and Japan. Many people live in these countries. In fact, China holds more people—over one billion—than any other country in the world.

The four main Japanese islands are part of a chain of recently formed volcanic mountains. Mountains cover two-thirds of the country.

Animals

Asia spreads from far northern lands covered with snow nine months a year to the steamy, hot rain forests that skirt the equator. This wide range of environments provides habitats for an enormous variety of animals.

Large white polar bears leap among the ice floes in the northernmost Siberian coasts. Reindeer, foxes, hares, and tiny, mouselike lemmings live in northern Asia. In northern China and Korea lives the thick-furred Siberian tiger, completely at home in cold and snow.

The forests of southern Asia swarm with animals—monkeys, tree-dwelling leopards, small herds of wild cattle called gaurs, and an ever-dwindling number of tigers. Indian elephants move through the forests in herds numbering from ten to fifty.

The deadly king cobra, the world's longest poisonous snake, also makes the forest its home. Its bite can kill a human within fifteen minutes. The cobra's enemy, the mongoose, also lives in the Asian forests. The fast, clever mongoose will attack and eat a cobra—or any other snake—on sight.

In the high bamboo forests in part of central China lives the giant panda. Mostly white with black legs, ears, and eye patches, this gentle bear-like creature is active mostly at night. The smaller red panda, which looks something like a raccoon, can be found in the Himalayas and the mountains of western China and northern Myanmar (Burma).

Imperial Eagle

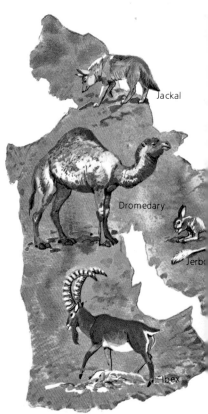

Jackal

Dromedary

Jerbo

Ibex

The largest horns grown by any animal are those of a sheep called the Pamir argali, or Marco Polo's argali. Marco Polo found this unusual creature during his travels across central Asia. The sheep's horns spiral outward and have been known to reach seventy-five inches (190.5 centimeters).

ASIA
Life on the Land

More than half the earth's people live on the vast continent of Asia. Throughout the world, people naturally tend to live in areas where the climate and land are good for producing food. About two-thirds of Asia's population make their living by farming, and the continent's agricultural areas are among its most crowded.

In much of China, Japan, India, and the tropical lands of Southeast Asia, the most important crop is rice. It is the main food of many Asian people, and Asia produces most of the world's rice. Cotton is the main crop of parts of south-western Asia, also known as the Middle East.

The land of northern Asia is too cold for much farming, and the soil in central Asia is not good for growing crops. In these regions, some people raise cattle and sheep.

Petroleum, or crude oil, is a precious substance in today's world. Beneath the deserts of the Middle East lie some of the world's greatest oil reserves. The countries of this region sell, or *export*, oil to many other countries around the world.

There is not much industry in most of Asia, but there is a lot in Israel, China, and western Russia. Industry in South Korea, Taiwan, Singapore, and Hong Kong is growing rapidly. Japan, which has few natural resources, continues to be a leader in world industry, producing automobiles, chemicals, and electronic equipment.

The Arabs of the Middle East tell a story about a young boy named Aladdin, who finds an old lamp. When he rubs the lamp, a genie appears and grants him three wishes.

Agricultural Area

Truck Farming

Vineyards

Sheep Raised

Jerusalem

Oil Fields

Dates

Farming by Irrigation

The Indonesian island of Bali, off of Southeast Asia, is known for its folk dances. One, called the *legong*, tells an ancient story of love and battle. Each movement has a meaning and tells a part of the story.

Mining

Fur Trapping

Logging

Truck Farming

Reindeer Herds

Rice Grown

Mining

Smelting of Ore

Truck Farming

Cossack Dancer

Logging

Mining

Wheatlands

Wheatlands

Light and Heavy Industry

Hydroelectric Power

Great Wall of China

Tea Grown

Citrus Fruits Grown

Sheep Raised

Gate of Heavenly Peace

Steel Manufactured

Goods Shipped by Caravan

Smelting of Ore

Farming

Chinese Junk

Ruins of Persepolis, Persia

Palace of the Dalai Lama

Traditional Chinese Urn

Agricultural Area

Agricultural Area

Corn

Persian Carpet

Cotton

Wheat

Bathing in the Sacred Ganges

Manufacturing

Cacao (Chocolate)

Cotton

Mt. Everest

Taj Mahal

Burmese Temples

Fishing

Coconuts

Rice Grown

Logging

Oil

Tea Grown

Coconuts

Agricultural Area

Fishing

Rubber

Teak

Coffee

ASIA
Countries and Cities

The nations of immense Asia tended to form in clusters. The continent has five large groupings of nations. The first, which borders the eastern edge of the continent, is called the Far East and its leading countries include China and Japan. Indochina and the islands of Indonesia make up the second group, and a third formed within the triangle of land which contains India. The desert countries make up a fourth cluster. Siberia, a part of northern Russia, stands alone as the fifth.

China holds the most people of any nation—over one billion. One out of every five persons on earth is Chinese!

With a history of more than five thousand years, Jerusalem has long been a holy city of Christianity, Judaism, and Islam. The city, divided after one war and reunified in another, was declared Israel's permanent capital in 1980.

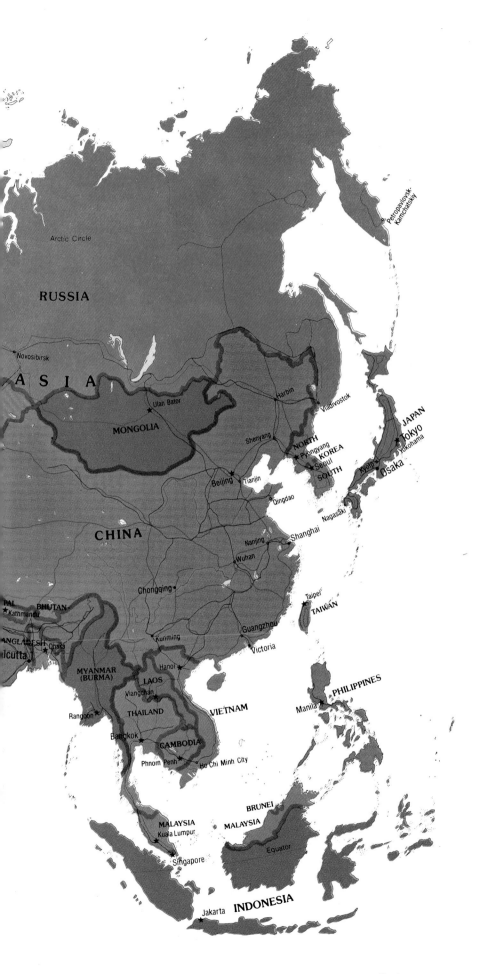

Roads
Railroads

But in terms of industry, Japan is a giant. The tiny island nation is one of the world's leading industrial powers.

The second cluster of countries occurs in Indochina. Many of the nations of Indochina formed around river valleys where food grows well. Myanmar (Burma) formed around the Irrawaddy River, and Thailand around the Menam. Cambodia and Vietnam share the lower Mekong River, while Laos grew around the northern part.

India, Pakistan, Bangladesh, and Sri Lanka, countries of the third grouping, struggle with poverty. Nearly 874 million people live in India, giving it a population second only to China's. Neighboring Bangladesh has fertile lands, but poor farming methods keep rice in short supply.

The fourth cluster of Asian nations lies on the deserts. Fewer people live here. Turkey, with more farmland than other countries in the region, has just fifty-nine million people. Only in Israel, established in 1948 as a Jewish homeland, does the population density approach that of European countries.

Siberia, the fifth region of Asia, is part of Russia. Its people are few and far between. Much of Russia's coal comes from the industrialized Kuznetsk Basin area, which also produces building materials, chemicals, and machinery.

Scale 1:42,000,000; one inch to 665 miles. Lambert's Azimuthal, Equal Area Projection
Elevations and depressions are given in feet

40,000 SQ MI
AREA

0   300   600
Miles

X-519695-26-11-19-15ᴾ-36ˣᴾ
COPYRIGHT BY
RAND McNALLY & COMPANY
MADE IN U.S.A.

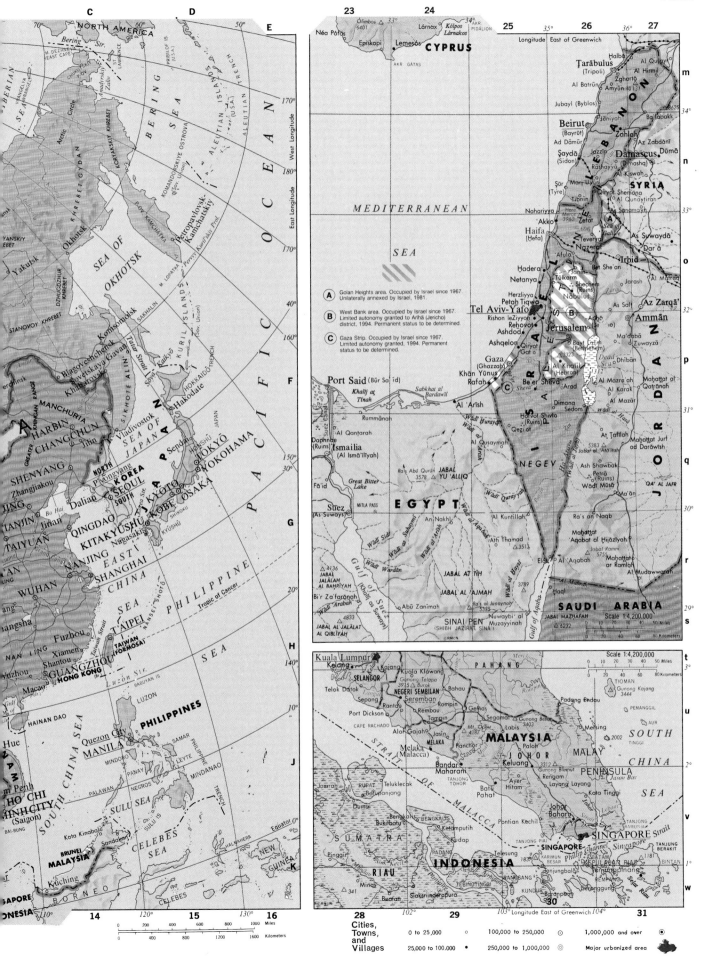

Golan Heights area. Occupied by Israel since 1967. Unilaterally annexed by Israel, 1981.

West Bank area. Occupied by Israel since 1967. Limited autonomy granted to Arīḥā (Jericho) district, 1994. Permanent status to be determined.

Gaza Strip. Occupied by Israel since 1967. Limited autonomy granted, 1994. Permanent status to be determined.

Scale 1:4,200,000

Cities, Towns, and Villages

0 to 25,000   100,000 to 250,000   1,000,000 and over

25,000 to 100,000   250,000 to 1,000,000   Major urbanized area

Africa
Terrain

Africa

Second largest continent

•

Third in population: 697,600,000

•

12 cities with over 2 million population

•

Highest mountain: Kilimanjaro, 19,340 feet (5,895 meters)

•

World's largest desert: Sahara, approximately 3,500,000 square miles (9,065,000 square kilometers)

•

World's longest river system: Nile, 4,145 miles (6,671 kilometers)

•

World's highest recorded temperature: Azizia, Libya, 136.4°F (58°C)

•

Equator passes through

The continent of Africa is second in size only to Asia. Yet few people realize just how huge it is. For example, the entire continental United States (which excludes Alaska and Hawaii) could be tucked comfortably into the Sahara Desert, which extends 3,200 miles (5,150 kilometers) across northern Africa.

Many people imagine Africa as a land of rain forests. In reality, most of Africa is covered with desert or grassland. The Sahara takes up most of northern Africa; the Kalahari and Namib deserts lie in the south. Between these two desert regions are many, many miles of grassland called *savanna*. Rain forests, following the equator, mainly occupy the middle of the continent.

Africa has some magnificent mountains, but it lacks the huge chains common to most of the other continents. The Atlas Mountains arch across the top of Africa, through Morocco, Algeria, and Tunisia, forming a barrier between the northern coast and the Sahara. They were raised over thirty million years ago, at the same time as the Alps of Europe.

In East Africa, mountain peaks follow two nearly parallel straight lines. Among the eastern mountains, snow-capped Mount Kilimanjaro, Africa's highest peak, soars to more than nineteen thousand feet.

Shown here is the type of grassland, called savanna, that covers much of Africa. This particular scene is in the nation of Zambia.

Africa's Great Rift Valley extends about four thousand miles (almost 6,500 kilometers). It can be traced along the many lakes and seas that fill parts of it. The cutaway at right shows some of those bodies of water.

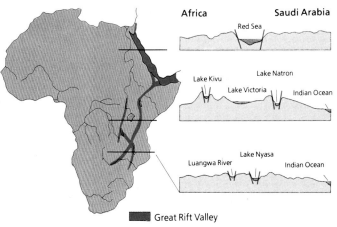

Between the peaks lies the Great Rift Valley. This is a long rip in the earth's surface where the land dropped down more than a mile (about one and a half kilometers).

The Drakensberg Mountains in southern Africa are the most unusual range on the continent. Actually, they are not true mountains, just tilted-up portions of the gigantic plateau that makes up Africa.

Four important rivers flow out of Africa. The Niger runs through several West African countries and out into the Atlantic Ocean. The Congo flows west out of central Africa. The Zambezi, toward southern Africa, flows east to the Indian Ocean. And finally, the great Nile flows northward through several countries, including Egypt, and empties into the Mediterranean Sea. The Nile is the longest river in the world.

Palm trees line the shore along the Gulf of Guinea, which lies to the south of Ghana. This coastal region sports white-sand beaches and blue lagoons.

AFRICA
Animals

Africa is a continent of rain forests, grassy plains, and deserts. Each environment holds different types of animals that have adapted to the conditions. Many African animals are beautiful creatures, but some of these magnificent beasts are in danger of becoming extinct.

In the north the enormous Sahara Desert spreads across thousands of miles. Not many animals can live in that wasteland, and those that do are able to survive with little or no water.

The best-known animal of the Sahara is the one-humped Arabian camel, also known as the dromedary. All camels in the Sahara are used as tame beasts of burden.

The great rain forest of central Africa straddles the equator. Within it roam bands of chimpanzees, which live on fruit and tender plants. The gorilla also lives here, a shy and gentle animal despite its size. Here, too, are found buffalo, leopards, many kinds of monkeys, and the little okapi, a brown-bodied animal with striped legs.

The vast, grassy plains that lie north and south of the central rain forests contain many of the continent's best-known animals. Herds of African elephants, the largest of all land animals, rumble across through the plains. The spotted cheetah, swiftest of all animals, prowls the grasslands in search of prey. It must compete with an even more famous cat, however, for the African lion, a symbol of pride and power, also hunts in the African plains.

Tarpon

Addax

Fennec

Pangolin

Colobus Monkey

Despite their fearsome appearance, gorillas are gentle beasts who eat only plants. Like many African animals, gorillas are threatened with extinction—a result of being hunted and losing their rain forest habitat.

Life on the Land

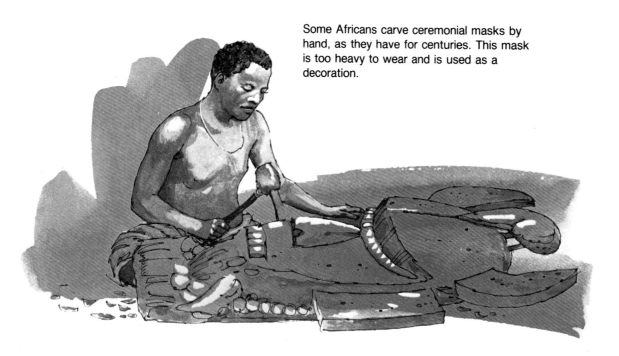

Some Africans carve ceremonial masks by hand, as they have for centuries. This mask is too heavy to wear and is used as a decoration.

Agricultural Area

Peanuts

Chocolate

Most Africans are either farmers or herders. Many of them live as their ancestors did for thousands of years. They roam the land for food or live in tiny villages, raising crops and animals mostly for their own use and not for sale to other countries.

Little farming can be done in hot, dry North Africa. But along the coasts of Morocco, Algeria, and Tunisia, farmers can grow a few crops—such as citrus fruits, grapes, almonds, grains, and olives.

Drilling for oil is important to several African countries. Algeria and Libya in the north and the nations of Nigeria and Gabon farther south export oil and natural gas to other countries.

West Africa is an important agricultural area. Among other crops, people here grow cacao beans, from which chocolate and cocoa are made. The forests of central Africa produce rubber trees and banana trees. In East Africa, herding cattle has been the main way of life for many years.

Farther south, in the country of South Africa, the fertile land is farmed by the descendants of Europeans who settled there many years ago. The land of South Africa also holds many minerals, such as platinum, antimony, chromium, and manganese. Most of the world's diamonds—both gems and those used in industry—and much of its gold come from South African mines. This vast mineral wealth helped build South Africa into the continent's most industrialized nation.

Ananse the Spider Man is a character in a famous African tale. Ananse gathered all the wisdom in the world into a huge pot and tried to keep it for himself. But the pot fell as Ananse tried to hide it in a tree, and all the wisdom blew away.

Agricultural Area

Moorish-style Architecture

Corn

Wheat

Vineyards

Olives

Fishing

Cairo

Sphinx

Nomad with Goats

Oil Fields

Tobacco

The Great Pyramid at Giza

Dates Harvested

Goods Shipped by Caravan

Sand Dunes

Cotton Grown

Cotton Made into Cloth

Leather Products Made

African Village

Palm Oil

Mining

Cattle Raised

Plantains (African Bananas)

Tourists Welcomed

Sheep Raised

Cattle Raised

ober

Cacao Beans (Chocolate)

Central Forests

Copra (Dried Coconut) Shipped

Oil Fields

Pygmy

Mt. Kilimanjaro

Minerals Mined

Masai Tribesman

Agricultural Area

Corn

Coal Mines

Victoria Falls

Tea

Diamond Mines

Citrus Fruits

Yams

Vanilla Beans Grown

Sheep Raised

Gold Mines

AFRICA
Countries and Cities

Human history began in Africa. Scientists believe that the earliest human beings walked the grasslands of East Africa about two million years ago. Over many years, humans migrated out of Africa to inhabit other parts of the world.

Civilization has a long history in North Africa. The Nile Valley of Egypt cradled the center of one of the world's oldest civilizations, which developed over five thousand years ago. Some of the cities of Egypt, including Alexandria and Cairo, are more than one thousand years old. Cairo is

Roads
Railroads

Country borders mean little to independent nomads like the Masai people. They cross the boundary between Kenya and Tanzania often in search of water and grazing lands for their cattle.

© 1979 Rand McNally & Co.
X-580000-279-2-3-2-4

Tunisia's population is concentrated along the coast, but village scenes such as this one are common in the nation's semi-arid mountain regions. Most of the inhabitants of these central and southern areas live in houses of stone and mud.

In many African nations, the capital city is the only sizable urban center. Harare, pictured here, is the capital and largest city of Zimbabwe, in southern Africa.

also the biggest city in Africa.

During the seventh century A.D., the religion of Islam was adopted throughout much of North Africa. Beautiful Muslim mosques were built in what is now Libya, Algeria, Tunisia, and Morocco.

By the 1400s, Europeans began sailing to Africa and conquering the peoples who lived there. The Europeans were interested mainly in profiting from the vast resources they found in Africa. By the early 1900s, almost all of Africa was under European rule. The borders of many African countries were set up by European colonists who settled there. Most of the European governments are gone now, replaced by the independent nations.

Much of West Africa is a hot, moist, lowland area. In past centuries raiders visited these shores, kidnaped people, carried them away in ships, and sold them as laborers throughout the world. Today, more than one-fourth of the people in Africa live in these western nations. Nigeria, with over 91 million people, is Africa's most populous country.

The equator passes through central Africa. Steamy Zaire, covered with rain forest, is the biggest country in the region, holding thirty-five million people.

Mountains and the Great Rift Valley separate East Africa from the rest of the continent. Here are grasslands on which groups of people herd cattle and many wild animals roam. Kenya and Tanzania have set aside vast areas where the animals are protected.

ATLANTIC OCEAN

ATLANTIC OCEAN

GULF OF GUINEA

Cities,
Towns,
and
Villages

0 to 25,000 ○	100,000 to 250,000 ⊙	1,000,000 and over ◉
25,000 to 100,000 •	250,000 to 1,000,000 ◎	Major urbanized area

Scale 1:16,850,000; one inch to 265 miles. Sinusoidal Projection
Elevations and depressions are given in feet

Longitude West of Greenwich   Longitude East of Greenwich

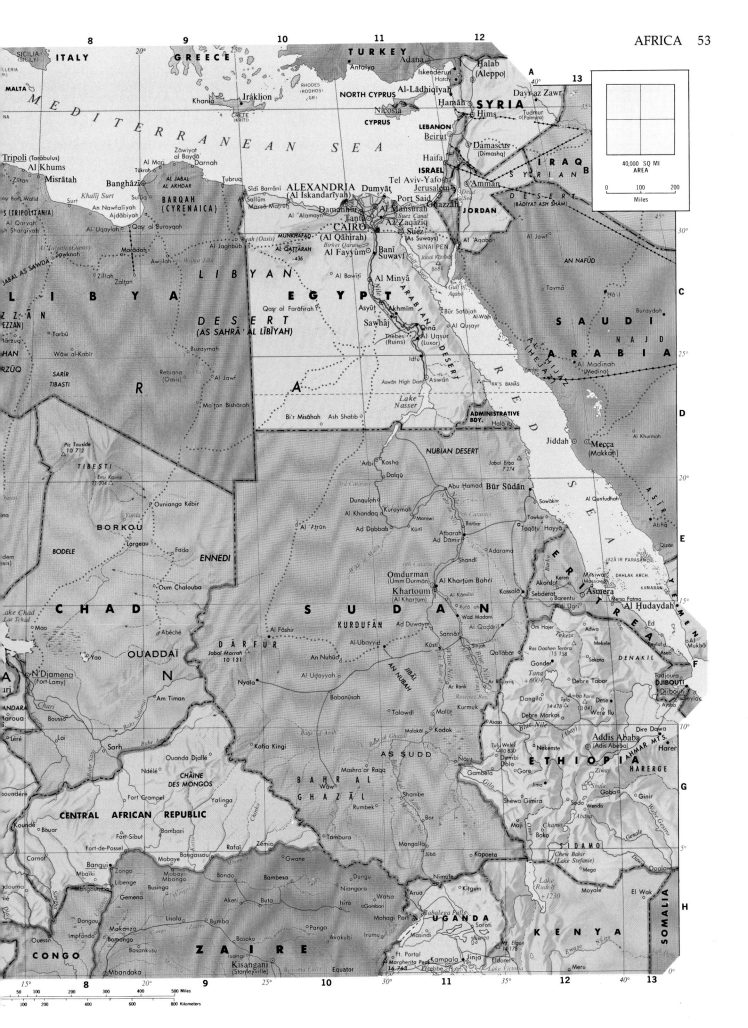

40,000 SQ MI
AREA

0   100   200
Miles

MEDITERRANEAN SEA

ITALY
SICILIA (SICILY)
MALTA

GREECE
Khaniá
Iráklion
CRETE (KRITI)
RHODES (RODHOS) (GR)

TURKEY
Antalya
Adana
Iskenderun
Hatay

Halab (Aleppo)
Dayr az Zawr
Al-Lādhiqīyah
Hamāh
Hims
Tudmur (Palmyra)
SYRIA
NORTH CYPRUS
Nicosia
CYPRUS
LEBANON
Beirut
Damascus (Dimashq)
IRAQ
SYRIAN
DESERT (BĀDIYAT ASH SHĀM)

Tripoli (Tarābulus)
Al Khums
Misrātah
Zlītan
Banī Walīd
Surt (TRIPOLITANIA)
Al Qaryah ash Sharqīyah

Zāwiyat al Baydā
Banghāzī
BARQAH (CYRENAICA)
AL JABAL AL AKHDAR
Darnah
Tubruq

Sīdī Barrānī
Sallūm
Marsá Matrūh
Al 'Alamayn

ALEXANDRIA (Al Iskandarīyah)
Dumyāt
Port Said
Damanhūr
Al Manṣūrah
Tanta
Az Zaqāzīq
CAIRO (Al Qāhirah)
Suez Canal
Suez (As Suways)
Al 'Aqabah

Haifa
Tel Aviv-Yafo
ISRAEL
Jerusalem
Ghazzah
JORDAN
Amman
Al Jawf
AN NAFŪD

Zillah
Zaltan
Marādah
Sowknah
JABAL AS SAWDA
An Nawfalīyah
Ajdābiyah
Al 'Uqaylah
Qaṣr al Burayqah

LIBYA

Awjilah
Al Jaghbūb
Sīwah (Oasis)
MUNKHAFAD AL QATTĀRAH 436

Al Jaghbūb
Birket Qarun
Al Fayyūm
Banī Suwayf

Jabal Katrīnah 8668
SINAI PEN.
Gulf of Aqaba
Taymā
Hā'il
Buraydah

LIBYAN DESERT (AS SAHRĀ AL LĪBĪYAH)

Al Bawītī
Al Minyā
Asyūt
Akhmīm
Qaṣr al Farāfirah

EGYPT

SAUDI ARABIA
AL HIJĀZ (HEJAZ)
NAJD
Al Madīnah (Medina)

Tarbū
Wāw al-Kabīr
Buzaymah
Sawhāj
Qinā
Thebes (Ruins)
Al Uqsur (Luxor)
Al Quṣayr

FEZZĀN
SARĪR TIBASTI
Rebiana (Oasis)
Al Jawf
Idfū
ARABIAN DESERT
Būr Safājah
Al Wajh
Al Khurmah

Ma'tan Bishārah
Aswān High Dam
Aswān
RA'S BANĀS

RED SEA

Pic Touside 10 712
Emi Koussi 11 204
TIBESTI

Bi'r Misāhah
Ash Shabb
Lake Nasser
ADMINISTRATIVE BDY.
Halā ib

Jiddah
Mecca (Makkah)
Al Khurmah
ASĪR

NUBIAN DESERT
'Arbī
Kosha
Dalqū
Jabal Erba 7 274
Abu Hamad
Būr Sūdān
Sawākin
Al Qunfudhah
Abha

Ounianga Kébir
Yarda
BORKOU
Largeau
Fada
Dunqulah
Al Khandaq
Kuraymati
Marawi
Kūrti
Barbar
Tawkar
Taqātu' Hayyā
JAZĀ'IR FARASĀN
Qīzān

BODÉLÉ
Oum Chalouba
ENNEDI
Al Atrūn
Ad Dabbah
Atbarah
Ad Dāmir
Adarama
DAHLAK ARCH.
Miṣiwa
Mersa Fatma
KAMARAN

Lake Chad
Lac Tchad
Mao
Abéché
CHAD

SUDAN
Omdurman (Umm Durmān)
Al Khartūm Bahrī
Shandī
Akordat
Keren
Aṣmera

Khartoum (Al Khartūm)
Al Kāmilin
Kassalā
Sebderat
Barentu
Al Ḥudaydah
YEMEN

CENTRAL AFRICAN REPUBLIC

DĀRFŪR
Jabal Marrah 10 131
KURDUFĀN
Al Fāshir
Al-Ubayyid
An Nuhūd
Al Uḍayyah
Ad Duwaym
Wad Madanī
Al Qaḍārif
Om Hajer
Adwa
Ras Dashen Terara 15 158
Mekele
DENAKIL
Ed
Mukhā

Yao
Nyala
Babanūsah
Sinjah
Qallābāt
Gonder
Tana 6004
Sekota
Aseb
ERITREA

N'Djamena (Fort-Lamy)
Am Timan
Talawdi
Malūt
Ar Ronk
Ar Ruṣayriṣ
Dangila
Amba Farit 14 478
Debre Tabor
Dese
Were Ilu
DJIBOUTI
Djibouti
Tadjoura
Seylac

ANDARA
Maroua
Bousso
Léré
Sarh
Ouanda Djallé
Kafia Kingi
Kodok
Malakal
Kurmuk
Asosa
Debre Markos
Blue Nile (Abay)
Tulu Welel 10 830
Dire Dawa
Harer
HARERGE

CHĀINE DES MONGOS
Yalinga
Mashra'ar Raqq
AS SUDD
Shambe
Nekemte
Dembi Dolo
Gore
ETHIOPIA
Jima
Shewa Gimira

Koundé
Bouar
Bambari
Rafaï
Zémio
Rumbek
Bor
Tambura
Mongalla
Jūbā
Gambela
Gilo
Maji
Bako
SIDAMO
Sodo
Wendo
Goba
Ginir
Wabe Gestro

Carnot
Fort-Sibut
Fort-de-Possel
Bangassou
Gwane
Nimule
Kapoeta
Chew Bahir (Lake Stefanie)
Chamo
Abaya
Genale

Banqui
Zongo
Mbaïki
Libenge
Mobaye
Bondo
Bambesa
Dungu
Arua
Kitgum
Lake Rudolf +1230
Mega
Moyale
El Wak
SOMALIA

Doumé
Mongoumba
Gemena
Businga
Akéti
Isiro
Gombari
Masindi
Soroti
Doolow

CONGO
Ouesso
Impfondo
Bomongo
Basankusu
Lisala
Bumba
Basoko
Panga
Avakubi
Irumu
Mahagi Port
UGANDA
Jinja
Kampala
Mt. Elgon 14 178
Eldoret
Meru
KENYA

ZAIRE
Mbandaka
Kisangani (Stanleyville)
Boyoma Falls
Murchison Falls
Ft. Portal
Margherita Peak 16 763
Entebbe
Lake Victoria
Equator

50   100   200   300   400   500 Miles
100   200   400   600   800 Kilometers

Scale 1:16,850,000 ; one inch to 265 miles. Sinusoidal Projection
Elevations and depressions are given in feet

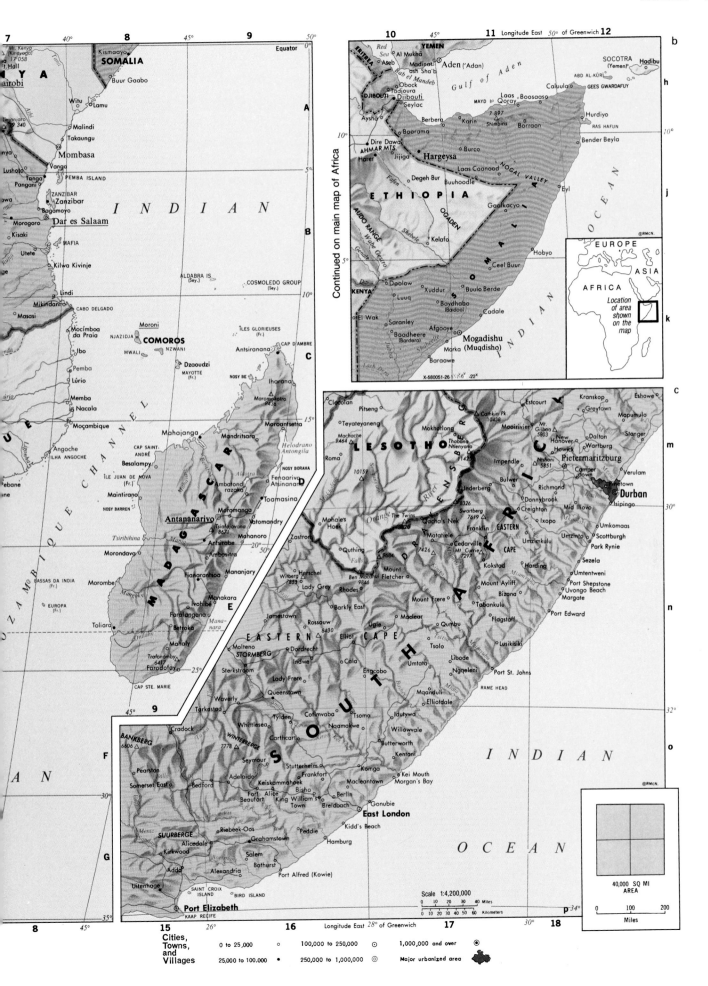

Continued on main map of Africa

EUROPE
ASIA
AFRICA
Location of area shown on the map

Cities, Towns, and Villages

0 to 25,000   100,000 to 250,000   1,000,000 and over

25,000 to 100,000   250,000 to 1,000,000   Major urbanized area

Scale 1:4,200,000

40,000 SQ MI
AREA

0   100   200
Miles

Oceania
Terrain

Deep in the heart of Australia, on the western plateau, lies Mount Olga. A worn-down collection of sandstone blocks, ''the Olgas'' and nearby Ayers Rock tower above the desert landscape.

A map of the world shows you just how big the Pacific Ocean is. It covers more than one-third of the earth's surface. You can also see that the ocean is full of islands of different sizes. Australia, New Zealand, and other islands in this region known as Oceania lie within the vast Pacific like stepping stones across a pond. Geographers group the islands into three regions. Polynesia includes Hawaii, Samoa, Tahiti, and Easter Island. Micronesia contains the Marshall, Caroline, and Gilbert islands. Melanesia includes the Fiji Islands and New Guinea.

Australia is the smallest continent. The Great Dividing Range thrusts its mountains along the eastern coast. In the south, it dips into the sea and rises up again to form Tasmania. Hammered by wind and water over hundreds of millions of years, the hump-shaped mountains of the Great Dividing Range are truly ancient.

West of the Great Dividing Range is the continent's great desert region. Australians call it the Outback. The mountains keep clouds and rain from moving into the Outback. Part of the Outback is bush country, where some trees and plants grow. The rest is made up of three deserts: the Great Sandy, the Gibson, and the Great Victoria.

The Cape York Peninsula is very different from the rest of Australia. Heat and rain combine to make ideal conditions for the tropical rain forests that grow there.

Perhaps the most famous region of Australia is not on the land, but in the ocean off the

northeastern coast. It is called the Great Barrier Reef. Built from colorful coral formations, it is the largest coral reef in the world and supports a great variety of ocean life.

Two main islands make up New Zealand: North Island and South Island. On the southwest coast of South Island, long, beautiful fjords cut into the land, just like the fjords of Norway. North Island boasts a volcanic region around Lake Taupo.

The Isle of Pines is one of several islands that make up New Caledonia. The culture and pleasant climate of this French territory attract many tourists.

Animals

Many of the animals of Australia are very different from those in other places. Australia was separated from all other parts of the world for about fifty million years, so its animals evolved in different ways, creating different solutions to the problems of survival. Most Australian *mammals*—furry, warm-blooded animals—are marsupials. Marsupials are animals like the kangaroo whose babies are kept in a pouch on the mother's body until they are old enough to care for themselves.

On the plains of Australia, several kinds of marsupials make their homes. Kangaroos live in little herds and eat grass. Some kangaroos can be as much as seven feet (over two meters) tall, but there are also small kangaroos called wallabies. Wombats look like beavers without tails. They dig tunnels that they sleep in during the day, and then forage for food at night. Ratlike, long-snouted bandicoots live much the same way as wombats.

Dingoes also roam the dry plains of Australia. When the first European settlers arrived, the dingo was the only large, meat-eating mammal on the continent. A member of the dog family, the dingo has long legs, a wolflike head, and yellow-red fur.

In the eastern part of Australia lives the koala. Koalas look like little bears, but in fact they are not. Unlike bears, which are mammals, koalas are marsupials and carry their young in pouches.

New Zealand does not have many animals that have not been brought by people. But on some islands near New Zealand live little reptiles called tuataras. They are the last survivors of a group of reptiles that lived about 225 million years ago—long before the rise of the dinosaurs.

Great numbers of sea creatures drift gracefully among the coral reefs and the deeper tropical waters surrounding the islands of Oceania. Most are brilliantly colored and very beautiful.

Blue Angelfish

Pacific Sheepshead

Albacore

Ocean Sunfish

Regal Angelfish

Sea Horse

Viperfish

Opah

Black Marlin

Triggerfish

Butterfly Fish

Emu

Frilled Lizard

Dingo

Death Adder

Echidna

Cassowary

Tree Kangaroo

Rabbit

Rock Wallaby

Womba

Great Gray Kangaroo

Kookaburra

Red Kangaroo

Koala

Platypus

Wandering Albatross

White Shark

Slender-billed Shearwater

Black Swan

The koala looks like a soft, cuddly teddy bear. Small, it weighs less than eighteen pounds (8.16 kilograms) when grown. For six months the cub rides in its mother's pouch. Later it rides on her back, even when she climbs high into the eucalyptus trees for the buds and leaves that are the koala's only food.

Dovey Petrel

Kiwi

Tuatara

Kea

Life on the Land

During the Age of Discovery, Europeans traveled to Australia, New Zealand, and other islands of Oceania. They settled the lands they found, and many descendants of Europeans remain on those lands.

Australia may be the smallest continent, but it is also one of the largest countries. Its population clings mostly to the coasts along the fertile lands of the east and southeast. Some people live at the edge of the Outback. They are mostly farmers who raise sheep and cattle. Australia's major exports include grain and wool. Today, Australia is highly industrialized.

New Zealand is not as industrialized as Australia, but manufacturing areas such as the paper industry are growing. The mild climate and excellent grazing land makes the raising of sheep and cattle very important in New Zealand.

Countries and Cities

The Land Down Under—that's what Australia and New Zealand are often called. The nickname grew out of the idea that these lands are directly opposite, that is, under the feet of, Europeans.

Australia is divided into states, and its people elect their leaders. New Zealand, also once a British colony, now operates in much the same way.

The islands of Oceania were once colonies, too, but have become nations. Western Samoa, Nauru, Fiji, the Solomon Islands, and the eastern half of New Guinea are now independent.

The descendants of Europeans who live in Australia and New Zealand speak English. There are groups of people in these places and on the surrounding islands who have lived there since ancient times, and most of them speak English, as well as the languages of their ancestors.

INDONESIA

Pasuruan

SUNDA

SUNDA TRENCH

INDIAN

OCEAN

Singaraja

Lombok Selat

Binjai

Mohamera 12 060

Lombok

SUMBAWA

Sumbawa Besar

FLORES

SUMBA

Waingapu

SAVU SEA

SAWU

ROTI

Kupang

TIMOR SEA

ALOR

LOMBLEN PANTAR

Dili

TIMOR

SELARU

ARAFURA SEA

TANJUNG VALS

C. VAN DIEMEN

DUNDAS

CROKER

MELVILLE

Van Diemen Gulf

BATHURST

Clarence Str.

Darwin

COBURG PEN.

WESSEL IS.

CAPE ARNHEM

ARNHEM LAND

Pine Creek

Blue Mud Bay

GROOTE EYLANDT

GULF

Anson Bay

Katherine

Limmen Bight

CARPENT

SIR EDWARD PELLEW GROUP

WELL

CAPE LONDONDERRY

Joseph Bonaparte Gulf

Wyndham

Birdum

Borroloola

Victoria River Downs

Daly Waters

Newcastle Waters

Burketown

Collier Bay

Mt. Hann 2800

KING LEOPOLD RANGES

NORTHERN

Alexandria

Da

BUCCANEER ARCH.

CAPE LEVEQUE

King Sd.

DAMPIER LAND

Derby

GEIKE RANGE

Fitzroy Crossing

Halls Creek

Tanami

TERRITORY

Tennant Creek

Camoowea

Mount Is

Broome

Fitzroy

Roebuck Bay

LaGrange

EIGHTY MILE BEACH

Barrow Creek

Q

LARREY POINT

RIPON

DeGrey

Port Hedland

DAMPIER ARCH.

MONTE BELLO IS.

BARROW

Roebourne

Marble Bar

GREAT SANDY DESERT

Mackay

Mt. Ziel 4955

MACDONNELL RANGES

Arltunga

Alice Springs

SIMPSON

NORTH WEST CAPE

Onslow

Millstream

Fortescue

HAMERSLEY RANGE

Nullagine

JAMES RANGE

DESERT

Birdsville

POINT CLOATES

Ashburton

Mt. Bruce 4024

Jiggalong

Macdonal

Charlotte Waters

Tropic of Capricorn

CAPE FARQUHAR

WESTERN

Disappointment

MUSGRAVE RANGES

Mt. Woodroffe 4970

Geographe

Carnarvon

Gascoyne

GIBSON DESERT

EVERARD RANGES

The Alberga

BERNIER

DORRE

Shark Bay

Peak Hill

Nabberu

Carnegie

Wells

Gillen

Oodnadatta

Eyre

DIRK HARTOG

STEEP POINT

Murchison

Meekatharra

Wiluna

AUSTRALIA

Carnegie

STUART RANGE

William Creek

Cue

Sandstone

Marree

Nannine

Mount Magnet

Yeo

Coopers Cr.

Austin

Laverton

SOUTH AUSTRALIA

Ajana

GREAT VICTORIA DESERT

Farina

HOUTMAN ROCKS

Northampton

Ballard

Carey

Ooldea Station

Torrens

Woomera

Geraldton

Mingenew

Barlee

Menzies

NULLARBOR

Hughes

Everard

Para

Dongara

Moore

Kalgoorlie

Rawlinna

PLAIN

Penong

Ceduna

Whyalla

Port Aug

Mullewa

Perenjori

Goddards Soak

Eucla

POINT FOWLER

EYRE PENINSULA

Port Pirie

Mifling

Goolgardie

Boulder

Lefroy

Moonta

Port W

Mopra

Lake Brows

Southern Cross

Cowan

Eyre

EYRE PENINSULA

Wallaroo

SWANLAND

Norseman

GREAT AUSTRALIAN BIGHT

Moonta

Ga

DARLING RANGE

Northam

York

Dundas

Salmon Gums

Port Lincoln

A

Perth

Narrogin

Ravensthorpe

Esperance

Gulf St.

Fremantle

Collie

Hopetoun

ARCHIPELAGO OF THE RECHERCHE

KANGAROO

Geographe Bay

Bunbury

Katanning

Busselton

CAPE JA

CAPE NATURALISTE

CAPE LEEUWIN

Nornalup

Albany

King George Sd.

Mt.

PT. D'ENTRECASTEAUX

WEST CAPE HOWE

INDIAN

OCEAN

40,000 SQ MI
AREA

0   100   200
Miles

A-590200-26-2-4-5-13
COPYRIGHT BY
RAND MCNALLY & COMPANY
MADE IN U.S.A.

Longitude East of Greenwich

Longitude East of Greenwich

Scale 1:16,850,000 ; one inch to 265 miles. Lambert's Azimuthal, Equal Area Project
Elevations and depressions are given in feet

North America
Terrain

North America

Third largest continent

•

Fourth in population: 453,300,000

•

28 cities with over 2 million population

•

Highest mountain: McKinley, 20,320 feet (6,194 meters)

•

World's largest island: Greenland

•

Location of North Magnetic Pole

North America has several mountainous areas. The western mountains are made up of two main chains that stretch from Alaska at the northern end of the continent to Panama at the southern end. The Rocky Mountains rise out of the Great Plains. The Rockies reach into Canada, where they are even more spectacular than they are in the United States.

The Great Basin lies between the two western mountain chains in the United States. Mountains prevent most of the Pacific moisture from reaching the Great Basin,

Coral reefs and submarine volcanoes formed the islands of the Caribbean. Many of the coral islands are flat and low-lying, while those of volcanic origin tend to be rugged. Shown here is volcanic Saba in the Leeward Islands.

© 1979 Rand McNally & Co.

Monument Valley lies on the border between Utah and Arizona. Here sandstone buttes, mesas, and arches rise above the sandy plain below—some as high as one thousand feet (three hundred meters).

British Columbia is the westernmost province of Canada. Its mountainous terrain once isolated it from the rest of the country. Today it is the site of several national parks, including Yoho National Park, shown here.

and the southern end of the basin is a desert. Farther south, a desertlike region covers much of the American Southwest and reaches deep into Mexico.

The two mountain chains extend into Mexico as well. The Sierra Madre Occidental is in the west, and the Sierra Madre Oriental is in the east. Plateau country spreads out between them, and it is here that most Mexicans live. Central America, at the south end of North America, is mainly mountainous.

The mountains of eastern North America are much lower than the ones to the west. Some of them are older mountains, and they have been worn down by time and weather. One such range is the Appalachians, the biggest mountain range in the eastern United States.

The Great Plains lie at the center of North America. This region is one of the largest plains on Earth, and the land is mostly flat or gently rolling as far as the eye can see.

North America has several important rivers and bodies of water. The Mississippi and Missouri rivers form the longest river system on the continent. Lake Superior, one of the five Great Lakes, is the largest freshwater lake in the world. The Panama Canal, near the southern tip of North America, is a human-made strip of water that allows ships to pass between the Atlantic and the Pacific oceans without having to go all the way around the southern tip of South America.

Animals

As the number of people in North America has increased, the number of wild animals has decreased. People have hunted some animals to extinction.

The buffalo, or American bison, was once nearly wiped out by hunters. The pronghorn antelope had a similar fate. Conservation efforts kept both species from extinction, and today they are found in protected areas on the Great Plains.

Wolves and mighty grizzly bears prowl in the north. The bald eagle, the national bird of the United States, is still found in the Northwest. These animals are endangered today.

The coyote, a symbol of the American West, preys on prairie dogs, mice, rabbits, and sometimes on livestock. Raccoons can be found from southern Canada to South America, except in parts of the Rockies and in deserts. Looking like a masked bandit, the raccoon forages at night and will feed on garbage. Both animals seem to thrive near people.

Many kinds of rattlesnakes, named for the rattles on their tails, inhabit North America. The largest of them is the eastern diamondback, often seven feet (over two meters) long. The coral snake, a colorful relative of the cobra, also lives in the deserts, as does a poisonous lizard called the Gila monster.

In the swamps and rivers of the southeastern part of the continent lives the alligator. These meat-eating reptiles can reach nine feet (2.7 meters) in length. Hunted for their skins, alligators are now protected.

It has been said that most of the animals that have ever lived on earth are now extinct. We know about prehistoric animals only from their fossil remains. Extinctions still occur, some of them the result of human interference. The passenger pigeon was seen and painted by John James Audubon in 1840.

Apatosaurus
135 Million Years Ago

Tyrannosaurus
70 Million Years Ago

Woolly Mammoth
10 Thousand Years Ago

Great Auk
Mid Nineteenth Century

Saber-Toothed Cat
1 Million Years Ago

Passenger Pigeon
Late Nineteenth Century

Grizzly Bear

Walrus

Herring Gull

Canada Goose

Polar Bear

Red Fox

Gray Wolf

Mountain Goat

Rock Ptarmigan

Beaver

Bald Eagle

Porcupine

Mountain Lion

Moose

Robin

Pronghorn

Gray Squirrel

King Salmon

Elk

White-tailed Deer

Raccoon

Willet

Sea Otter

Bison

Cottontail

Gambel's Quail

Diamondback Rattlesnake

Opossum

Turkey

California Sea Lions

Peccary

Alligator

Armadillo

Roseate Spoonbill

Brown Pelican

Squirrel Monkey

Gray Whale

NORTH AMERICA
Life on the Land

Ice hockey is a popular sport played by both amateurs and professionals in Canada and the United States, as well as in other countries. Hockey is the national sport of Canada.

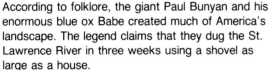

According to folklore, the giant Paul Bunyan and his enormous blue ox Babe created much of America's landscape. The legend claims that they dug the St. Lawrence River in three weeks using a shovel as large as a house.

The United States and Canada, two of the three largest countries in North America, are also among the richest nations in the world. Many factors contribute to this abundant wealth, including agriculture. North America has much fertile farmland and a good climate for growing a variety of crops.

Rich mineral deposits also contribute to the prosperity of the United States and Canada. Mineral exports from these countries include copper, lead, asbestos, zinc, silver, nickel, coal, crude oil, and natural gas.

North America's rich forests and mineral reserves have helped the United States and Canada to become world leaders in manufacturing. Many cities in these countries have been huge industrial centers for many years, but this is gradually changing.

Agriculture is very important in Mexico and in other countries of North America as well. Corn is grown in Mexico. In Central America and the islands called the West Indies, coffee, sugarcane, and bananas are grown. But much of the land in these countries is not good for growing crops, and many of the farmers do not have modern machinery.

There is not as much manufacturing in the other countries of North America, although the iron, steel, and chemical industries are growing. Mexico is also a leading producer of silver and petroleum. Tourists, interested in the country's sunny climate and ancient ruins, also help the economy.

Greenland

Canneries

Mining

Alaskan
Pipeline

Oil Fields

Salmon Fishing
and Canning

Lumbering

Fur Trapping

Totem Pole

Fishing

Ski Trails

Lumbering

Canadian Wheatlands

Agricultural Area

Giant Redwoods

Potatoes

Wheat

Dairyland

Mt. Rushmore

Statue of Liberty

Offshore Oil Drilling

Truck Farming

Hollywood

Soybeans

Agricultural Area

Cars
Manufactured

Washington, D.C.

Citrus Groves

Corn

Longhorn Cattle

Peanuts

Tobacco

Agricultural Area

Cape Canaveral

Cotton

Citrus Groves

Corn

Sugarcane

Olmec Sculpture

Oil Fields

The famous Ballet Folklorico of
Mexico performs many dances
based on Mexican history and
legend. The dancers here wear
costumes modeled after those
worn by the Mayas, an Indian
people who lived in Mexico a
thousand years ago.

Ruins of Ancient Pyramids

Agricultural Area

Sugarcane Made
into Molasses

Coffee

Bananas

Countries and Cities

Mexico City is the capital and fastest-growing city of that nation. It is among the five most populous cities of the world. In 1985, the city suffered a major earthquake, which caused much damage and killed thousands.

Of all the continents, the boundaries between countries are the simplest in North America. Most of the continent is divided among three nations: Canada, the United States, and Mexico. Central America, considered a part of North America, covers an area less than a third the size of Mexico and contains seven countries.

The countries of North America are mainly inhabited by descendants of Europeans who crossed the seas after the 1500s. Native Americans, the people who lived here long before the Europeans arrived, still populate some areas and many live close to the way their ancestors lived.

Like the people of the continent's three largest nations, most North Americans elect their leaders. In some countries, such as Panama, military leaders have taken control of the government. For Panama, at least, this may now be changing. Cuba, an island nation in the Caribbean, has long had a communist government.

The main language of each North American nation is the language spoken in the European country that once dominated the area. For example, Spain once ruled Mexico, and although Mexico is now independent, its people still speak Spanish.

Cities usually grow up around areas that are accessible to trade routes, and the cities of North America are no exception. Many of them sprung up near bodies of water that were traveled by the many traders who explored the land. For example, Chicago, Illinois, grew up on a

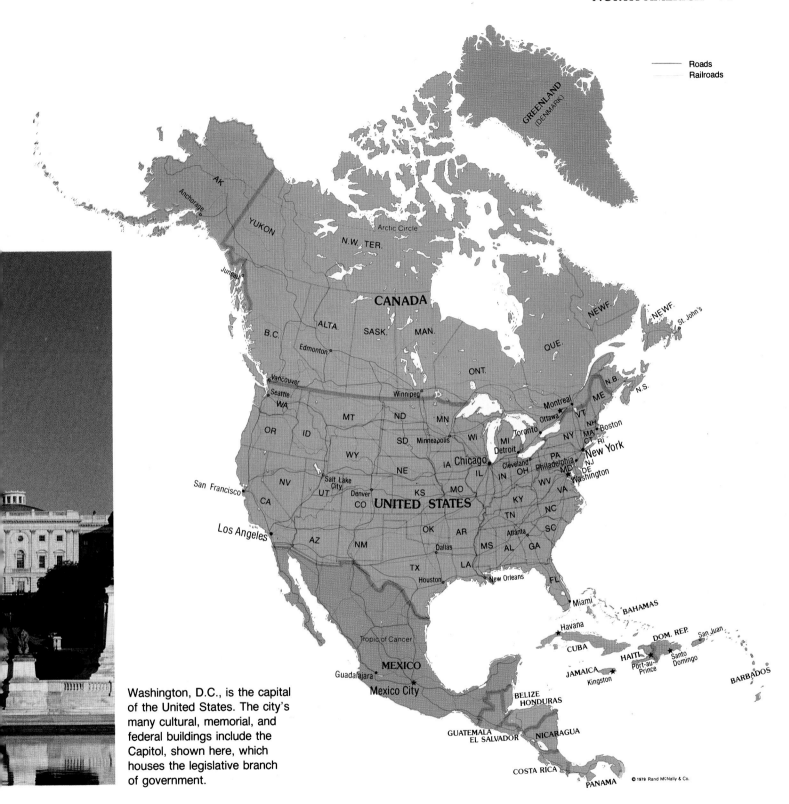

Roads
Railroads

Washington, D.C., is the capital of the United States. The city's many cultural, memorial, and federal buildings include the Capitol, shown here, which houses the legislative branch of government.

crossroads that linked the Great Lakes and the Mississippi River. Detroit, Toronto, Ottawa, and Cleveland have a similar history.

Today, some of the biggest and most modern cities in the world are in North America. The population of New York City is one of the largest in the world. With over 8.8 million people, Mexico City is even larger. In fact, Mexico is the most populous Spanish-speaking country in the world and carries much influence with those nations.

Cities,
Towns,
and
Villages

0 to 25,000 ○   100,000 to 250,000 ◎   1,000,000 and over ◉

25,000 to 100,000 •   250,000 to 1,000,000 ◉   Major urbanized area

Scale 1:12,600,000; one inch to 200 miles. Conic Projection
Elevations and depressions are given in feet

Longitude West 105° of Greenwich

INSET MAP:

QUEBEC

Gulf of St. Lawrence

CAPE BAULD

Strait of Belle Isle

LONG RANGE MTS.

White Bay

Notre Dame Bay

C. ST. JOHN

GROS MORNE NAT'L PARK

Deer Lake

Botwood

Windsor

Gander

Corner Brook

Stephenville

Grand Falls

Bonavista

TERRA NOVA NAT'L PARK

Trinity

Bonavista Bay

C. ST. GEORGE

Red Indian Lake

NEWFOUNDLAND

St. George's Bay

St. George's

Cabot Strait

CAPE RAY

Channel-Port-aux-Basques

Grand Bank

Fortune Bay

Burin

Placentia Bay

St. John's

CAPE NORTH

CAPE BRETON ISLAND

ST. PIERRE AND MIQUELON (Fr.)

ATLANTIC OCEAN

Same scale as main map

©RMCN

MAIN MAP LABELS:

FRANKLIN

BAFFIN ISLAND

MELVILLE PENINSULA

Foxe Basin

PRINCE CHARLES ISLAND

BAFFIN NAT'L PARK

Pangnirtung

PENN.

Nettilling

Cumberland Sound

C. MERCY

Arctic Circle

Amadjuak

Iqaluit

HALL PEN.

Frobisher Bay

Lake Harbour

EVERETT MTS.

RESOLUTION

KILLINIQ I.

SOUTHAMPTON ISLAND

Foxe Channel

SALISBURY

Hudson Strait

C. DE NOUVELLE-FRANCE

C. HOPES ADVANCE

AKPATOK

FOXE PEN.

C. LOW

COATS

MANSEL

NOTTINGHAM ISLAND

BELL PEN.

Ivujivik

PENINSULE D'UNGAVA

Ungava Bay

TORNGAT MTS.

Nain

Hebron

Hopedale

NEWFOUNDLAND

Makkovik

Rigolet

Hamilton Inlet

Cartwright

Roes Welcome Sound

FISHER STRAIT

KEEWATIN

Povungnituk

OTTAWA ISLANDS

HUDSON BAY

All islands within bays and straits lie within Northwest Territories.

Minto

Michikamau L.

Happy Valley Goose Bay

Ashuanipi

MEALY MTS.

Battle Harbour

LONG RANGE MTS.

Strait of Belle Isle

BELCHER ISLANDS

LABRADOR

Schefferville

Churchill Falls

Petitsikapau

Lac Joseph

GROS MORNE NAT'L PARK

Corner Brook

Stephenville

St. George

Ft. Severn

C. HENRIETTA MARIA

PTE. LOUIS-XIV

La Grande

QUEBEC

MTS. OTISH

Manicouagan

ILE D'ANTICOSTI

James Bay

Chisasibi

AKIMISKI I.

Opinaca

Eastmain

Natashquan

Little Mecatina

Romaine

Gulf of St. Lawrence

Severn

Winisk

Ft. Albany

Moosonee

Mistassini

Nemiscau

Chibougamau

St. Felicien

Roberval

Chambord

Dolbeau

Alma

Kenogami

Clarke City

Sept-Iles

ILES DE LA MADELEINE

ONTARIO

Attawapiskat

Coral Rapids

Fraserdale

La Sarre

Rouyn

Amos

Senneterre

Val-d'Or

Malartic

St. Maurice

Parent

La Tuque

Chicoutimi

Jonquiere

Baie Comeau

Baie St. Paul

Matane

MTS. CHIC-CHOCS

Cap Chat

Ste. Anne des Monts

PEN. DE GASPE

Gaspe

Chandler

Carlisle

Bonaventure

Baraquet

Bathurst

CHAUTAUS BAY

St. Joseph

Nakina

Hearst

Kapuskasing

Cochrane

Iroquois Falls

Timmins

Kirkland Lake

Matagami

Ville-Marie

Temiscaming

Shawinigan

Grand-Mere

Trois-Rivieres

Drummondville

Victoriaville

Levis

Quebec

Rimouski

Riviere-du-Loup

Edmundston

NEW BRUNSWICK

Campbellton

Newcastle

Richibucto

PRINCE EDWARD ISLAND

Summerside

Charlottetown

KOUCHIBOUGUAC NAT'L PARK

Armstrong Sta.

Geraldton

Longlac

Oba

Chapleau

Cobalt

North Bay

Pembroke

Renfrew

Ottawa

Hull

Joliette

Sorel

St. Hyacinthe

Sherbrooke

Granby

MAINE

Woodstock

Fredericton

Moncton

Amherst

Truro

New Glasgow

Antigonish

Port Hawkesbury

Sydney

CAPE BRETON HIGHLANDS NAT'L PARK

NOVA SCOTIA

St. Troat L.

Sioux Lookout

Dryden

Lac Seul

Nipigon

Marathon

PUKASKWA NAT'L PARK

Sudbury

Sturgeon Falls

Mattawa

Huntsville

Bancroft

Smiths Falls

Brockville

Kingston

Alexandria Bay

FUNDY NAT'L PARK

Saint John

St. Andrews

St. Stephen

Bay of Fundy

VERMONT

NEW HAMPSHIRE

Concord

Portland

Digby

Kentville

Windsor

Dartmouth

Halifax

Bridgewater

Lunenburg

Liverpool

Shelburne

CAPE SABLE

Yarmouth

e of the Woods

Rainy

Thunder Bay

Lake Superior

MICHIPICOTEN I.

Sault Ste. Marie

Thessalon

Espanola

Blind River

Parry Sound

Georgian Bay

MANITOULIN

Owen Sound

Wiarton

Midland

Barrie

Orillia

Lindsay

Peterborough

Trenton

Belleville

Cobourg

Lake Ontario

Rochester

Niagara Falls

BUFFALO

NEW YORK

Albany

MASS.

CONN.

R.I.

Providence

Hartford

CAPE COD

CANADA

U.S.A.

Le Frontiere

ATLANTIC OCEAN

Ogdensburg

Valleyfield

Champlain

Plattsburgh

Montpelier

BOSTON

Duluth

Superior

Marquette

Escanaba

Green Bay

MINNESOTA

WISCONSIN

MICHIGAN

Madison

St. Paul

MINNEAPOLIS

MILWAUKEE

CHICAGO

ILLINOIS

Lake Michigan

Saginaw Bay

Saginaw

Flint

Lansing

Grand Rapids

DETROIT

Windsor

Leamington

Toledo

OHIO

Sarnia

Chatham

London

St. Thomas

Port Huron

Kincardine

Kitchener

St. Catharines

Hamilton

TORONTO

Oshawa

Whitby

Lake Simcoe

Lake Huron

Lake Erie

PENNSYLVANIA

Scranton

NEW YORK

NEW YORK

N.J.

MONTREAL

St. Lawrence River

Lake Nipissing

COORDINATE LABELS:

14 15 16 17 18 19 20 21 23

80° 75° 70° 65° 60° 55°

60° Longitude West of Greenwich 55°

Arctic Circle

B C D E F G h k

65° 60° 55° 50° 45° 40°

12 15 16 17

SCALE:

0 25 50 75 100 200 300 400 500 Miles

0 100 200 400 600 800 Kilometers

H-520200-26- 4-9-8-18

COPYRIGHT BY

RAND McNALLY & COMPANY

MADE IN U.S.A.

40,000 SQ MI AREA

0 100 200

Miles

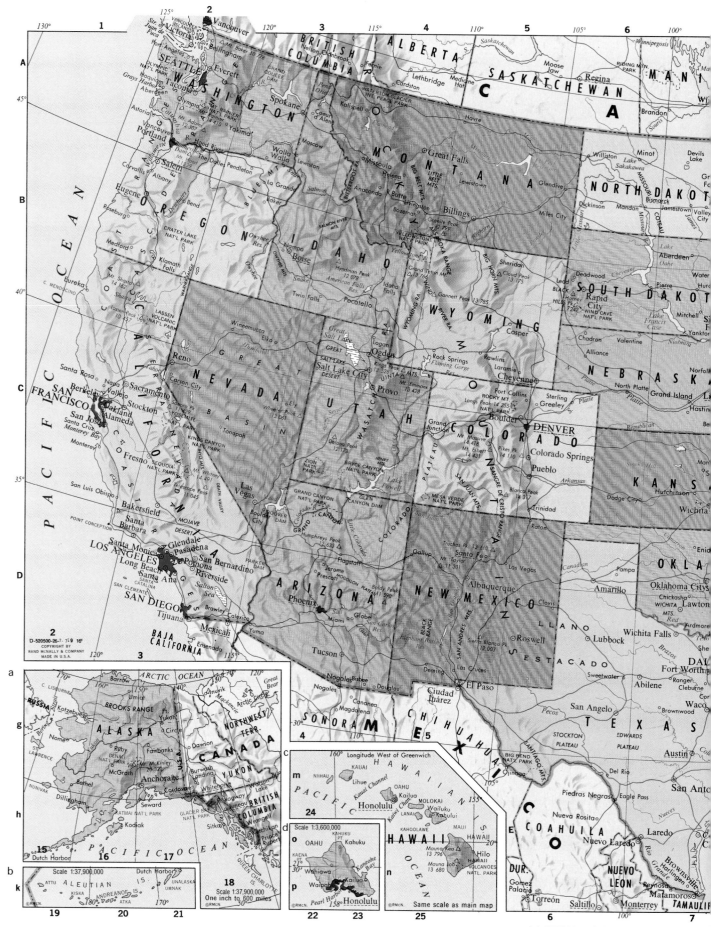

Scale 1:12,600,000; one inch to 200 miles. Polyconic Projection

Elevations and depressions are given in feet

PANAMA

Scale 1:1,080,000

Scale 1:17,200,000; one inch to 270 miles. Polyconic Projectio

Elevations and depressions are given in feet

Inset maps

Puerto Rico inset
ATLANTIC OCEAN

Arecibo   San Juan

Aguadilla   Bayamón   CABEZAS DE   ST. THOMAS   TORTOLA
PTA. HIGUERO   SAN JUAN   (U.S.A.)
Utuado   Fajardo   CULEBRA   Charlotte   ST. JOHN
Mayagüez   **PUERTO RICO**   Caguas   Amalie   (U.S.A.)
(U.S.A.)   Coamo   Cayey   Humacao   Vieques
Ponce   Salinas   Guayama   VIEQUES

CABO ROJO   CARIBBEAN   SEA   Christiansted

SAINT CROIX
(U.S.A.)

Mona Passage

Scale 1:4,300,000

0   10   20   30   40 Miles
0 10 20 30 40 50 60 Kilometers
©RMcN

St. Thomas inset
LITTLE
HANS LOLLICK
INNER BRASS   OUTER BRASS   HANS LOLLICK
STORMY PT   PICARA PT   GRASS
THATCH CAY   CAY
ST. THOMAS
(U.S.A.)
Crown Mt.   Charlotte Amalie
1558   (St. Thomas)
WATER   Nadir
FLAMINGO PT   St. Thomas
©RMcN   Harbor   Scale 1:5,400,000

Main map labels

W.VIRGINIA   Roanoke   Richmond
VIRGINIA   Chesapeake Bay
Norfolk
Raleigh
NORTH CAROLINA
Mt. Mitchell   Charlotte
6684   CAPE HATTERAS
SOUTH
CAROLINA   Wilmington
Columbia   CAPE FEAR
Augusta
GEORGIA   Charleston
Savannah
Jacksonville
St. Augustine
Ocala
FLORIDA
Tampa
Tampa Bay   CAPE CANAVERAL

W. Palm Beach
MIAMI   GRAND BAHAMA   GREAT ABACO
CAPE SABLE   Lake Okeechobee
Key West   Nassau   BAHAMAS
Straits of Florida   ANDROS   CAT
LONG   SAN SALVADOR (WATLING)
HAVANA   Guanabacoa   Matanzas
Marianao   Cárdenas   ELEUTHERA
del Río   Santa Clara   ACKLINS
Cienfuegos   Sancti Spíritus   CAICOS
CUBA   Ciego   Nuevitas   (Br.) TURKS
Trinidad   de Avila   Camagüey   GT. INAGUA
ISLA   Manzanillo   Holguín
DE LA   Sierra Maestra   PUNTA
JUVENTUD   Guantánamo   MAISÍ
GRAND CAYMAN   Cap-Haïtien   Puerto Plata
(Br.)   C. CRUZ   Santiago   Santiago de los   28 374
de Cuba   Caballeros   Sánchez
WINDWARD PASSAGE   GONÂVE   SAMANA
Montego Bay   Mt. Denham   ÎLE DE LA   C. SAMANA
2236   Port Antonio   GONÂVE   ENGAÑO
Spanish Town   HAITI   Pico Duarte   DOMINICAN
JAMAICA   Kingston   Port-au-Prince   3417   REPUBLIC
Santo Domingo
HISPANIOLA
GREATER ANTILLES

NORTH AMERICAN BASIN

ATLANTIC OCEAN

PUERTO RICO TRENCH

Mayagüez   VIRGIN IS.   Anguilla
San Juan   (Br.)
Ponce   Charlotte Amalie   BARBUDA
PUERTO RICO   (Ant.)
(U.S.A.)   SAINT CROIX   ANTIGUA
(U.S.A.)   AND
Mona Passage   ST. KITTS AND NEVIS   BARBUDA
MONTSERRAT   Pointe-à-Pitre
(Br.)   V. Soufrière   GUADELOUPE
4869   (Fr.)
Basse-Terre
DOMINICA

MARTINIQUE (Fr.)
Fort-de-France

WINDWARD IS.   ST. LUCIA
ST. VINCENT
AND THE   BARBADOS
GRENADINES
Kingstown   Bridgetown

LESSER   ANTILLES

GRENADA

CARIBBEAN   SEA

PUNTA DE GALLINAS   ARUBA   SAN ROMAN   TOBAGO
PENÍNSULA   (Neth.)   CURAÇAO BONAIRE
DE GUAJIRA   (Neth.) (Neth.)   ISLA LA   TRINIDAD AND TOBAGO
Golfo de   PEN. DE   Willemstad   TORTUGA
Venezuela   PARAGUANÁ   ISLA DE   Port of Spain
Santa Marta   Coro   MARGARITA   TRINIDAD
Barranquilla   Ciénaga   Maracaibo   San Felipe   Carúpano
Cartagena   Soledad   Cabimas   Puerto   La Guaira   Cumaná
Lago de   Cabello   CARACAS   Puerto
AMERICA   Maracaibo   Maracay   la Cruz
Barquisimeto   Valencia   Maturín
José   Limón   Barinas   Trujillo   El Tigre
Cartago   Golfo de los   Colón   Lorica   Sincelejo   Mompós   Calabozo   Ciudad Guayana   Morawhanna
RICA   Mosquitos   PANAMA   Golfo   Magangué   Valera   Guanare   Cerro Bolívar
David   ISTMO   del Darién   Montería   Mérida   Puerto de   San Fernando   Ciudad Bolívar
PANAMA   Antón   Ocaña   Nutrias   de Apure
PEN. DE   Golfo de   Cúcuta   San Cristóbal   VENEZUELA   Cerro Icutú
AZUERO   Panamá   Pamplona   7800
COIBA   Barrancabermeja   Bucaramanga   Arauca
Medellín   Tunja   GUYANA
Sonsón   Meta
Manizales   COLOMBIA
ISLA DE   Pereira   Armenia   SANTA FE DE   San Fernando   BRAZIL
MALPELO   Ibagué   BOGOTÁ   de Atabapo   SERRA PACARAIMA
(Colombia)   Buenaventura   Girardot
Cali   Palmira   Villavicencio

Scales and legends

50   100   200   300   400   500 Miles
100   200   400   600   800 Kilometers

Cities and Towns
0 to 50,000   ○   500,000 to 1,000,000   ◎
50,000 to 500,000   ☉   1,000,000 and over

13

40 000 SQ MI
AREA

0   100   200
Miles

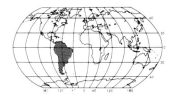

Fourth largest continent

•

Fifth in population: 313,900,000

•

14 cities with over 2 million population

•

Highest mountain: Aconcagua,
22,831 feet (6,959 meters)

•

World's highest waterfall: Angel Falls,
3,212 feet (979 meters)

•

Equator passes through

South America
Terrain

Kaieteur National Park in central Guyana lies in a region of forested highlands and plateaus. Wind and water have molded the park's sandstone and shale into a variety of interesting formations.

The Sierra of Peru is a high-altitude region of gentle slopes surrounded by the towering peaks of the Andes. Farmland is found between the mountains; this is a farming community near the Urubamba River.

The Andes Mountains run down the entire western side of South America. Stretching more than four thousand miles (about 6,500 kilometers), the Andes chain is the longest in the world. This range also has some of the world's tallest peaks. Only the Himalayas in Asia are higher than Argentina's Mount Aconcagua.

Where Argentina, Bolivia, and Chile meet, the Andes split into two ranges. They are separated by a plateau about four hundred miles (about 650 kilometers) wide. This is called the Altiplano, or high plateau.

In northern Chile, between the Andes and the Pacific, is the Atacama Desert. This de-sert is near the ocean, yet it is one of the driest spots on earth. In some parts of the Atacama, no rainfall has ever been recorded.

Many rivers and streams tumble from the Andes and other highland areas. The Amazon River begins in the An-des of Peru and flows almost four thousand miles (more than six thousand kilometers) to the Atlantic Ocean. The Amazon contains more water than any other river on earth. Over four million cubic feet (more than 113,000 cubic me-ters) pour out of the Amazon and into the Atlantic each sec-ond. The stream of fresh water from the river can be detected in the ocean for about a hun-

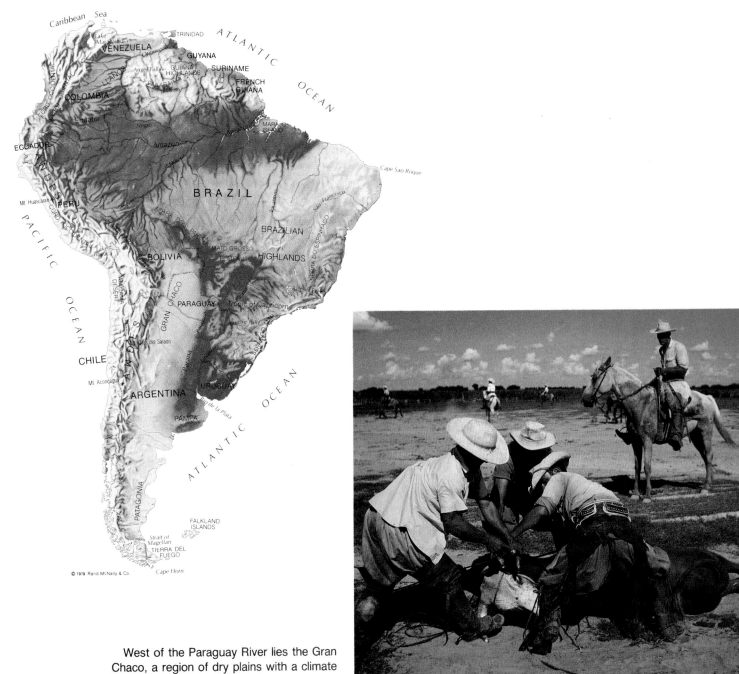

West of the Paraguay River lies the Gran Chaco, a region of dry plains with a climate harsher than that of eastern Paraguay. The nation's large cattle ranches are found here.

dred miles (160 kilometers) off the coast of South America.

The Amazon flows out of a huge plain called the Amazon River basin, an area almost as big as the United States. The equator runs through this area, so it is very warm, and it re- ceives a lot of rainfall. These factors combine to make this region the biggest tropical rain forest on earth.

A plain stretches across Par- aguay and most of Argentina. It is made up of two different areas—the Gran Chaco and the Pampa. The Gran Chaco is a dry region with few trees. The Pampa receives more rain; it is a nearly treeless grassland ideal for grazing cattle and sheep. Patagonia lies near the southern tip of South America.

SOUTH AMERICA
Animals

Nearly a fourth of all the species of animals known live in South America. But as in other parts of the world, people are hunting these animals and attempting to develop the lands the animals live on, so many creatures are in danger of becoming extinct.

The Amazon rain forests provide homes for many animals. The jaguar, a big spotted cat, prowls among the trees at night, and herds of piglike peccaries root in the underbrush. The tapir, an animal that looks like a large hog with a long nose, also lives in the forest.

The trees of the rain forest brighten with the colorful plumage of parrots, macaws, toucans, and other birds. Monkeys howl and shriek from the treetops. Sloths hang upside down from the branches and feed on leaves at night. The boa constrictor also lives in the rain forest.

In the rivers swim caimans, the alligators of South America. Schools of razor-toothed fish called piranha cruise through the water.

On the plains of South America live giant anteaters, which may be more than six feet (about two meters) long. The long-legged maned wolf live here, too.

In the Andes live llamas, vicuñas, and alpacas. Some of these animals have been tamed by people who use them like sheep or cattle. The spectacled bear lives on mountain slopes. It gets its name from the circles of yellowish fur, like eyeglass frames, around its eyes.

The mysterious Galapagos Islands lie about 600 miles (965.58 kilometers) off the coast of Ecuador. Here live rare cormorants that cannot fly, great lizardlike iguanas, and giant turtles weighing 500 pounds (226.8 kilograms). Some species have been victimized by overhunting, but the islands are now a national park and wildlife refuge.

Sloth

Tapir

Manatee

Scarlet Ibis

Coatimundi

Ocelot

Piranha

Toucan

Green Turtle

Spectacled Bear

Llama

Spider Monkey

Red Brocket Deer

Anaconda

Vampire Bat

Capybara

Jaguar

Howling Monkey

Macaw

Chinchilla

Great Anteater

Vicuña

Condor

Guanaco

Maned Wolf

Brazilian Lapwing

Alpaca

Pampas Deer

Blue Marlin

Torrent Duck

Rhea

Elephant Seal

Magellan Goose

Magellan Penguin

Cavy

Black-necked Swan

Sperm Whale

SOUTH AMERICA
Life on the Land

Close to half of all South Americans make their living by farming. Most farms are quite small and can produce only enough food for the families that own them. Most of these people use old-fashioned ways of farming, with no machinery. There are huge modern farms and ranches, however, and they are owned by a small number of wealthy people. Some of these farms are larger than many of the states of the United States. The farms grow huge quantities of coffee, cacao, wheat, sugar, bananas, rice, and other food.

The rain forests—hot, moist, and thick with vegetation—might seem to be an ideal place for farming. But, cleared of trees, the jungle soil loses the important nutrients crops need to grow. Much of the rain forest has been cut down in a futile attempt to create farmland. Herds of sheep and beef cattle are raised on giant ranches. Argentina is one of the largest producers of beef in the world.

Drilling rigs in Venezuela and Ecuador jab into the earth and bring up crude oil. These two nations are the largest oil exporters in South America.

Life in the big cities of South America is much like life in the cities of North America. There are tall, modern buildings, airports, and busy streets. But many of the Indians outside of the cities of Peru, Bolivia, and Ecuador still live the way their ancestors lived. And in the rain forest, some people live as they have for thousands of years.

Over four hundred years ago, the empire of the Incas thrived in the Andes. Legend has it that the first Incas, Manco Capac and his sister, were created from the sun god on the Isle of the Sun in Lake Titicaca.

Weaving is an age-old art in the Andes, one passed down from generation to generation. Indians spin thick alpaca wool into yarn to make warm blankets, hats, and other clothing.

Soccer, or *fútbol* in Spanish, is one of the world's most widely played sports. It is the national sport of several South American countries.

Oil Exported

Oil Fields

Mining

Coffee Bean
Farming

Emerald Mining

Fishing

Shipping

Agricultural Area

The Amazon

Rubber

Brazil Nuts
Harvested

Cotton

Mahogany
Logging

Spanish-style
Architecture

Indians of Peru

Agricultural Area

Machu Picchu
(Inca Ruins)

Fishing in
Lake Titicaca

Soccer

Brasilia

Mining

Anchovy Fishing

Mining

Light Industry

Rio de Janeiro

Trees Tapped
for Tannin

Copper

Coffee Grown

Agricultural Area

Cattle Raising

Beef for Export

Fishing

Wheatlands

Bonito Fishing

Lumbering
and Sawmills

Sheep Herding

SOUTH AMERICA
Countries and Cities

Ancestors of Native Americans crossed a narrow bridge of land between what is now Alaska and Siberia thousands of years ago. Over the centuries, the American Indians populated all of North and South America. In the Andes Mountains, a sophisticated Native American group called the Incas thrived and created a huge empire. The lands that now make up the nations of Peru, Ecuador, and Bolivia were part of the empire. Cuzco, Peru, was its capital.

Just like North America, South America was explored and conquered by Europeans after about 1500. People from Spain, Portugal, and other European countries took over the land, some of which had been inhabited by Indians for centu-

Roads
Railroads

Suriname's bauxite deposits fuel the nation's mining and industry. Much of the bauxite is shipped to the United States, but Suriname's factories also process the ore into alumina and aluminum for export.

ries. Many wars were fought over the years, but the borders of many of today's South American countries have existed for over one hundred years.

South America's largest and most populated country is Brazil. More people live in Brazil than in all other South American countries combined. Brazil is also the continent's leading industrial nation. Argentina is the second-largest South American country.

Like North Americans, most South Americans speak the language of the European country that once ruled the area in which they live. For example, Brazil was once a colony of Portugal, and today most Brazilians speak Portuguese. Many other South American countries were once dominated by Spain, and Spanish is widely spoken on the continent. There are many American Indians in South America who still speak the languages of their ancestors.

South America has many important cities. The biggest of them is São Paulo, Brazil—one of the largest cities in the world. Buenos Aires, Argentina, and Rio de Janeiro, Brazil, are also in the world's top ten in population. All three cities are very modern and have a lot of industry. If you look at these three cities on the map, you see they all have something in common: they are all near the Atlantic coast. They all grew up around or very close to natural ports, or places where ships could safely land.

Inhabited before the eleventh century, Quito, Ecuador, is situated in the Andes, only fifteen miles (twenty-four kilometers) south of the equator. The city is the capital and second largest city in Ecuador.

The second largest city in Brazil and one of the most populous in the world, Rio de Janeiro is a popular tourist destination.

86

Cities and Towns

0 to 50,000	○
50,000 to 500,000	○
500,000 to 1,000,000	◉
1,000,000 and over	⬤

Scale 1:16,850,000; one inch to 265 miles. Sinusoidal Project
Elevations and depressions are given in feet

Scale 1:4,200,000

Miles
0 10 20 30 40
0 10 20 30 40 50 60
Kilometers

H-549100-26 5-8-10-19"
COPYRIGHT BY
RAND McNALLY & COMPANY
MADE IN U.S.A.

Longitude West 65° of Greenwich

Tropic of Capricorn

BOLIVIA
PARAGUAY
BRAZIL
ARGENTINA
CHILE
URUGUAY

Grid columns: 2 · 3 · 4 · 5 · 6 · 7 · 8
Rows: A · B · C · D · E · F · G · H

70° · 65° · 60° · 55° · 50° · 45°
20° · 25° · 30° · 35° · 40° · 45° · 50° · 55°

Chile / Pacific coast
Tocopilla · Antofagasta · ATACAMA TRENCH · Pedro de Valdivia · Mejillones · Calama · Chuquicamata · PUNA DE ATACAMA · Taltal · 25 050 · Chañaral · Caldera · Copiapó · Huasco · Vallenar · Freirina · Coquimbo · La Serena · Tongoy · Ovalle · Illapel · Los Vilos · Quillota · Viña del Mar · Valparaíso · San Antonio · Melipilla · SANTIAGO · San Bernardo · Rancagua · San Fernando · Curicó · Constitución · Talca · Cauquenes · San Carlos · Parral · Linares · Talcahuano · Concepción · Chillán · Coronel · Lota · Los Angeles · Lebu · Angol · Victoria · Lautaro · Temuco · Valdivia · Corral · La Unión · Osorno · Puerto Varas · Puerto Montt · Ancud · Castro · ISLA DE CHILOÉ · ARCHIPIÉLAGO DE LOS CHONOS · Golfo Corcovado · PENÍNSULA DE TAITAO · Golfo de Penas · ARCHIPIÉLAGO MADRE DE DIOS · HANOVER · WELLINGTON · CAMPANA · Puerto Aisén · Golfo San Jorge · SANTA INÉS · PEN. DE BRUNSWICK · Punta Arenas · Puerto Natales · DESOLACIÓN · TIERRA DEL FUEGO · CORD. DARWIN · HOSTE · NAVARINO · ISLAS DIEGO RAMIREZ · CABO DE HORNOS (CAPE HORN) · ISLA DE LOS ESTADOS

Argentina (north / Andes)
Tupiza · Tarija · Villazón · Yacuiba · La Quiaca · Orán · Tartagal · JUJUY · Jujuy · San Pedro · SALTA · Salta · Metán · San Antonio de los Cobres · Nevados de Cachi 22 047 · Cachinal · Llullaillaco 22 057 · Salar de Arizaro · Cerro Azufre (Copiapó) Vol. 19 947 · Cerro Bonete 22 541 · Tinogasta · CATAMARCA · Andalgala · Cerro Aconcagua 22 835 · Uspallata Pass 12 540 · Portezuelo de Tucuman Vol. 22 310 · Cerro Mercedario 22 211 · Chilecito · LA RIOJA · La Rioja · SIERRA DE FAMATINA · Catamarca · Tucumán · TUCUMAN · Monteros · Bella Vista · SANTIAGO DEL ESTERO · Santiago del Estero · Frías · Salinas Grandes · Añatuya · Dean Funes · Cruz del Eje · Villa Dolores · SAN JUAN · San Juan · San Felipe · MENDOZA · Mendoza · SANTIAGO · CORDOBA · Córdoba · Alta Gracia · Villa María · Río Tercero · San Luis · SAN LUIS · Villa Mercedes · Río Cuarto · Mercedes · Maipo (Vol.) 17 464 · San Rafael

Gran Chaco / northeast
GRAN CHACO · CHACO · FORMOSA · Formosa · Presidencia Roque Sáenz Peña · Resistencia · Villa Angela · Corrientes · CORRIENTES · SANTA FE · Santa Fe · Paraná · ENTRE RÍOS · Goya · Reconquista · Vera · Tostado · Rafaela · San Francisco · Esperanza · Rosario · San Nicolás · Zárate · Pergamino · Junín · Lincoln · Venado Tuerto · Laboulaye · Cañada de Gómez · Casilda · Gálvez · Victoria · Gualeguay · Concepción del Uruguay · Gualeguaychú · Concordia · Salto · Paysandú · Colón

Paraguay
Puerto Olimpo · Bella Vista · Porto Murtinho · Mariscal Estigarribia · Puerto Casado · Pedro Juan Caballero · Concepción · Horqueta · Pedro P. Peña · Villa Hayes · Asunción · Luque · San Pedro · Coronel Oviedo · Villarrica · Caazapá · San Juan Bautista · Pilar · Encarnación · Humaitá

Uruguay
URUGUAY · MONTEVIDEO · Salto · Paysandú · Mercedes · Fray Bentos · Trinidad · Durazno · Florida · Minas · Rocha · Maldonado · Colonia · Rivera · Tacuarembó · Melo · Treinta y Tres · Santa Vitória do Palmar

Brazil (southeast)
MINAS GERAIS · BELO HORIZONTE · São José do Rio Prêto · Franca · Ribeirão Prêto · Ouro Prêto · João del Rei · Barbacena · Juiz de Fora · SÃO PAULO · SÃO PAULO · RIO DE JANEIRO · Araçatuba · Araraquara · Bauru · Lins · Campinas · Jundiaí · Taubaté · Sorocaba · Santos · São Vicente · Piracicaba · PARANÁ · Londrina · Ponta Grossa · Curitiba · Paranaguá · Castro · São Francisco do Sul · Joinville · SANTA CATARINA · Blumenau · Itajaí · Brusque · Florianópolis · Tubarão · Laguna · RIO GRANDE DO SUL · Caxias do Sul · Passo Fundo · Erechim · Carazinho · Lajes · São Leopoldo · PORTO ALEGRE · Santa Maria · Cachoeira do Sul · Bagé · Pelotas · Rio Grande · MISSIONES · Posadas · Cruz Alta · Uruguaiana · SERRA GERAL · SERRA DO MAR

Patagonia
LA PAMPA · Santa Rosa · General Pico · General Acha · Guatraché · Trenque Lauquen · Nueve de Julio · Bragado · Chivilcoy · Mercedes · Chascomús · Dolores · General Madariaga · BUENOS AIRES · Olavarría · Azul · Tandil · SIERRA DEL TANDIL · Necochea · Mar del Plata · Balcarce · Lobería · Tres Arroyos · Coronel Dorrego · Bahía Blanca · SIERRA DE LA VENTANA · Coronel Suárez · Coronel Pringles · Juárez · Rauch · Ayacucho · Saavedra · NEUQUÉN · Neuquén · Zapala · General Roca · RÍO NEGRO · Choele Choel · Carmen de Patagones · Viedma · San Antonio Oeste · Golfo San Matías · PENÍNSULA VALDÉS · PTA. DELGADA · Puerto Madryn · Trelew · Rawson · CHUBUT · Esquel · San Carlos de Bariloche · Nahuel Huapi · Gastre · MESETA DE SOMUNCURÁ · LOMAS COLORADAS · Comodoro Rivadavia · Golfo San Jorge · CABO DOS BAHIAS · PAMPA DE CASTILLO · Colhué Huapi · Lago Buenos Aires · C. BLANCO · Puerto Deseado · PUNTA MEDANOSA · SANTA CRUZ · GRAN BAJO · San Julián · MESETA DE LAS VIZCACHAS · Lago San Martín · Lago Viedma · Lago Argentino · Puerto Santa Cruz · Bahía Grande · Río Gallegos · Estrecho de Magallanes · Río Deseado · Río Chico

Falkland / Atlantic
FALKLAND IS. (ISLAS MALVINAS) (Br.) (Claimed by Argentina) · Stanley · BANCO BURDWOOD · Estrecho de Le Maire

ATLANTIC OCEAN · PACIFIC OCEAN

Tropic of Capricorn

Inset — Buenos Aires (Scale 1:1,080,000)
RÍO DE LA PLATA · Tigre · San Fernando · San Isidro · Vicente López · Olivos · Villa Ballester · General Sarmiento · General San Martín · Villa de Mayo · Morón · San Justo · Lanús · Avellaneda · Sarandí · Bernal · Quilmes · Berazategui · Lomas de Zamora · Banfield · Temperley · Almirante Brown · Florencio Varela · Esteban Echeverría · Burzaco · Longchamps · Ezeiza · Moreno · Merlo · Libertad · González Catán · Mariano Acosta · Ituzaingó · Hurlingham · Caseros · Garín · José C. Paz · Bella Vista · Canal Punta Indio · General Las Heras
Scale 10 Miles · 16 Kilometers
34° 30' · 34° 45' · 58° 45' · 58° 15'
k · m · n

Inset — Rio de Janeiro (Scale 1:1,080,000)
SERRA DAS ARARAS · Teresópolis · Pedra do Sino 7605 · Cascatinha · Dedo de Deus 5705 · Petrópolis · Guapimirim · SERRA DO COUTO · RIO DE JANEIRO · Pedro do Rio · Paquequer Pequeno · Avelar · Itaipava · Pati do Alferes · Miguel Pereira · Vassouras · Barão de Juperaná · Governador Portela · Sacra Família do Tinguá · Paracambi · Japeri · Mendes · Queimados · Seropédica · Nova Iguaçu · Belford Roxo · Mesquita · Coelho da Rocha · Nilópolis · São João de Meriti · Duque de Caxias · Pavuna · São Mateus · Olinda · Realengo · Anchieta · Campo Grande · Santa Cruz · Jacarepaguá · Pedra Branca 3360 · Pico da Tijuca 3349 · Corcovado 3300 · RIO DE JANEIRO · Niterói · São Gonçalo · Sete Pontes · Neves · Magé · Imbariê · Guia de Pacobaíba · ILHA DO GOVERNADOR · Baía de Guanabara · Cava · Seruí · Itambí · Inhomirim · Copacabana · PONTA DO ARPOADOR · Baía de Sepetiba · PONTA DO MARISCO · PONTA DA PRAIA FUNDA · ISLA REDONDA · ATLANTIC OCEAN
Scale 10 Miles · 16 Kilometers
22° 30' · 23° · 43° 30' · 43°
o · p · q
9 · 10 · 11 · 12 · 13 · 14 · 15

Scale / legend
40,000 SQ MI AREA · 0 · 100 · 200 Miles
Scale 1:17,200,000; one inch to 270 miles. Sinusoidal Projection
Elevations and depressions are given in feet
0 · 50 · 100 · 200 · 300 · 400 · 500 Miles
0 · 100 · 200 · 400 · 600 · 800 Kilometers
Longitude West of Greenwich
H-549200-26

Antarctica
The South Pole

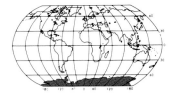

Antarctica

Fifth largest continent

•

No permanent population

•

Highest mountain: Vinson Massif, 16,864 feet (5,140.14 meters)

•

Location of South Pole

•

Location of South Magnetic Pole

•

World's lowest recorded temperature: Vostok, -129°F (-89°C)

Antarctica, the coldest continent on earth, rests squarely on the South Pole. It is so cold here that a person without the right kind of clothing would freeze to death in a matter of minutes. In midwinter, which is June in the Southern Hemisphere, temperatures may drop below −100° F (−73° C).

Like some places north of the Arctic Circle, Antarctica is without sunlight for part of the year. This happens because the earth's spin axis, which runs through the North and South poles like the axle of a wheel, tilts into the plane of the planet's orbit. A visitor at the South Pole would enjoy six months of never-ending daylight during the summer— and six months of frigid, never-ending night during winter.

Even in the summer the sun gives the continent little heat. Most of Antarctica is covered with snow heaped so thick it forms a mile-high plateau at the pole.

Microscopic creatures teem in the waters around Antarctica, but large animals can be found there as well. Among these are seals, birds, and the 150-ton (135-metric-ton) blue whale.

Antarctica is the home of many penguins. Though penguins are birds, they cannot fly. Their wings are used as paddles to help them move underwater.

In 1911, explorers discovered the South Pole. Today, no one makes a permanent home on this frozen continent, but hundreds of scientists study Antarctica's unique environment.

Penguins frolic in the cold waters off the coast of Antarctica. These are adélie penguins, one of only two species that breed in Antarctica.

World Facts and Comparisons

General Information

Mean distance from the earth to the sun, 93,020,000 miles.

Mean distance from the earth to the moon, 238,857 miles.

Equatorial diameter of the earth, 7,926.38 miles.

Polar diameter of the earth, 7,899.80 miles.

Mean diameter of the earth, 7,917.52 miles.

Equatorial circumference of the earth, 24,901.46 miles.

Polar circumference of the earth, 24,855.34 miles.

Total area of the earth, 197,000,000 square miles.

Total land area of the earth (incl. inland water and Antarctica), 57,900,000 square miles.

Highest elevation on the earth's surface, Mt. Everest, Asia, 29,028 feet.

Lowest elevation on the earth's land surface, shores of the Dead Sea, Asia, 1,312 feet below sea level.

Greatest known depth of the ocean, southwest of Guam, Pacific Ocean, 35,810 feet.

Area of Africa, 11,700,000 square miles.

Area of Antarctica, 5,400,000 square miles.

Area of Asia, 17,300,000 square miles.

Area of Europe, 3,800,000 square miles.

Area of North America, 9,500,000 square miles.

Area of Oceania (incl. Australia) 3,300,000 square miles.

Area of South America, 6,900,000 square miles.

Population of the earth (est.1/1/95), 5,628,000,000.

Principal Islands and Their Areas

Island	Area (Sq.Mi.)
Baffin I., Can.	195,928
Borneo (Kalimantan), Asia	287,300
Celebes (Sulawesi), Indon.	73,057
Corsica, France	3,352
Crete, Greece	3,189
Cuba, N.A.	42,800
Cyprus, Asia	3,572
Great Britain, U.K.	88,795
Greenland, N.A.	840,000
Hainan Dao, China	13,100
Hawaii, U.S.	4,034
Hispaniola, N.A.	29,300
Hokkaidō, Japan	32,245
Honshū, Japan	89,176
Iceland, Europe	39,800
Ireland, Europe	32,600
Jamaica, N.A.	4,200
Java (Jawa), Indon.	51,038
Luzon, Philippines	40,420
Madagascar, Africa	227,000
Mindanao, Philippines	36,537
Newfoundland, Can.	42,031
New Guinea, Oceania	309,000
Puerto Rico, N.A.	3,500
Sakhalin, Russia	29,500
Sardinia, Italy	9,301
Sicily, Italy	9,926
Southampton I., Can.	15,913
Spitsbergen, Norway	15,260
Sri Lanka, Asia	24,900
Taiwan, Asia	13,900
Tasmania, Austl.	26,200
Tierra del Fuego, S.A.	18,600
Vancouver I., Can.	12,079
Victoria I., Can.	83,897

Principal Lakes, Oceans, Seas, and Their Areas

Lake/Country	Area (Sq.Mi.)
Arabian Sea	1,492,000
Arctic Ocean	5,400,000
Atlantic Ocean	31,800,000
Baltic Sea, Eur.	163,000
Bering Sea, Asia-N.A.	876,000
Black Sea, Eur.-Asia	178,000
Caribbean Sea, N.A.-S.A.	1,063,000
Caspian Sea, Asia-Europe	143,240
Chad, L., Cameroon-Chad-Nig.	6,300
Erie, L., Can.-U.S.	9,910
Great Salt Lake, U.S.	1,680
Hudson Bay, Can.	475,000
Huron, L., Can.-U.S.	23,000
Indian Ocean	28,900,000
Mediterranean Sea, Eur.-Afr.-Asia	967,000
Mexico, Gulf of, N.A.	596,000
Michigan, L., U.S.	22,300
North Sea, Eur.	222,000
Ontario, L., Can.-U.S.	7,540
Pacific Ocean	63,800,000
Red Sea, Afr.-Asia	169,000
Superior, L., Can.-U.S.	31,700
Tanganyika, L., Afr.	12,350
Titicaca, Lago, Bol.-Peru	3,200
Victoria, L., Ken.-Tan.-Ug.	26,820
Yellow Sea, China-Korea	480,000

Principal Mountains and Their Heights

Mountain/Country	Elev. (Ft.)
Aconcagua, Cerro, Arg.	22,831
Annapurna, Nepal	26,504
Apo, Mt., Phil.	9,692
Ararat, Turkey	16,804
Blanc, Mont (Monte Bianco), France-Italy	15,771
Bolívar (La Columna), Ven.	16,411
Cameroon Mtn., Cam.	13,451
Chimborazo, Ecuador	20,561
Cook, Mt., New Zealand	12,349
Cristóbal Colón, Pico, Colombia	19,029
Dhaulāgiri, Nepal	26,810
Elbert, Mt., Co., U.S.	14,431
El'brus, Russia	18,510
Elgon, Mt., Kenya-Uganda	14,178
Etna, Mt., Italy	10,902
Everest, Mt., China-Nepal	29,028
Fairweather, Mt., Canada-U.S.	15,300
Fuji-san, Japan	12,388
Gannett Pk., Wy., U.S.	13,785
Gongga Shan, China	24,790
Grand Teton Mtn., Wy., U.S.	13,766
Grossglockner, Austria	12,457
Hood, Mt., Or., U.S.	11,239
Illimani, Nevado, Bol.	21,151
Iztaccíhuatl, Mex.	17,159
Jaya, Puncak, Indon.	16,503
Jungfrau, Switz.	13,642
K2 (Godwin Austen), China-Pak.	28,250
Kānchenjunga, India-Nepal	28,208
Kātrīnā, Jabal, Egypt	8,668
Kenya, Mt., Kenya	17,058
Kilimanjaro, Tanzania	19,340
Kommunizma, Pik, Tajikistan	24,590
Kosciusko, Mt., Austl.	7,316
Koussi, Emi, Chad	11,204
Lassen Pk., Ca., U.S.	10,457
Logan, Mt., Canada	19,524
Longs Pk., Co., U.S.	14,255
Margherita, Zaire-Uganda	16,763
Matterhorn, Italy-Switz.	14,692
Mauna Kea, Hi., U.S.	13,796
Mauna Loa, Hi., U.S.	13,680
McKinley, Mt., Ak., U.S.	20,320
Misti, Volcán, Peru	19,098
Mulhacén, Spain	11,424
Nānga Parbat, Pak.	26,660
Nevis, Ben, U.K.	4,406
Ólimbos, Greece	9,570
Orizaba, Pico de, Mex.	18,406
Pikes Pk., Co., U.S.	14,110
Popocatépetl, Volcán, Mex.	17,887
Rainier, Mt., Wa., U.S.	14,410
Sajama, Nevado, Bol.	21,463
Shasta, Mt., Ca., U.S.	14,162
Toubkal, Jebel, Morocco	13,665
Triglav, Slovenia	9,393
Vesuvio (Vesuvius), Italy	4,190
Vinson Massif, Antarc.	16,864
Washington, Mt., N.H., U.S.	6,288
Whitney, Mt., Ca., U.S.	14,491
Wilhelm, Mt., Pap. N. Gui.	14,793

Principal Rivers and Their Lengths

River/Continent	Length (Mi.)
Amazonas-Ucayali, S.A.	4,000
Amu Darya, Asia	1,578
Amur, Asia	2,744
Arkansas, N.A.	1,459
Brahmaputra, Asia	1,770
Colorado, N.A. (U.S.-Mex.)	1,450
Columbia, N.A.	1,200
Congo (Zaïre), Africa	2,900
Danube, Europe	1,776
Euphrates, Asia	1,510
Ganges, Asia	1,560
Huang (Yellow), Asia	3,395
Indus, Asia	1,800
Irrawaddy, Asia	1,300
Lena, Asia	2,700
Limpopo, Africa	1,100
Loire, Europe	625
Mekong, Asia	2,600
Mississippi, N.A.	2,348
Missouri, N.A.	2,315
Murray, Australia	1,566
Negro, S.A.	1,300
Niger, Africa	2,600
Nile, Africa	4,145
Ohio, N.A.	981
Orange, Africa	1,300
Orinoco, S.A.	1,600
Paraguay, S.A.	1,610
Paraná, S.A.	2,800
Peace, N.A.	1,195
Pechora, Europe	1,124
Plata-Paraná, S.A.	3,030
Red, N.A.	1,270
Rhine, Europe	820
Rhône, Europe	500
Rio Grande, N.A.	1,885
Salween (Nu), Asia	1,750
São Francisco, S.A.	1,988
Saskatchewan-Bow, N.A.	1,205
Snake, N.A.	1,038
St. Lawrence, N.A.	800
Sungari (Songhua), Asia	1,140
Syr Dar'ya, Asia	1,370
Tarim, Asia	1,328
Tennessee, N.A.	652
Tigris, Asia	1,180
Tocantins, S.A.	1,640
Ucayali, S.A.	1,220
Ural, Asia	1,509
Uruguay, S.A.	1,025
Volga, Europe	2,194
Xingú, S.A.	1,230
Yangtze (Chang), Asia	3,900
Yellowstone, N.A.	671
Yenisey, Asia	2,543
Yukon, N.A.	1,770
Zambezi, Africa	1,700

Index

Map Names and Abbreviations

This table lists the names and the abbreviations used for features on the physical-political maps. Each entry includes the feature name, the language from which it comes, and in the case of foreign names, its English translation. Abbreviations are shown for those names that are abbreviated on the maps.

Ákra (Greek): cape, *Akr.*
Cabo (Spanish, Portuguese): cape, *C.*
Cap (French): cape, *C.*
Cape (English): *C.*
Cerro (Spanish): mountain, hill
Cordillera (Spanish): mountain chain, *Cord.*
Erg (Arabic): strait
Estrecho (Spanish): strait
Fort (English): *Ft.*
Golfo (Spanish, Italian): gulf, bay, *G.*
Gora (Russian): mountain, *G.*
Gulf (English): *G.*
Hai (Chinese): sea
Île (French): island
Ilha (Portuguese): island
Isla (Spanish) island, *I.*
Jabal (Arabic): mountain
Khrebet (Russian): mountain range
Lake (English): *L.*
Lago (Spanish, Portuguese): lake, *L.*
More (Russian): sea
Mountain(s) (English): *Mt. (Mts.)*
Mys (Russian): cape, *M.*
National (English): *Nat'l.*
Occidental (Spanish): western

Oriental (Spanish): eastern
Óros (Greek): mountain
Ozero (Russian): lake, *Oz.*
Peninsula (English): *Pen.*
Peski (Russian): desert
Plato (Russian): plateau
Point (English): *Pt.*
Pointe (French): point, *Pte.*
Poluostrov (Russian): peninsula, *P-Ov.*
Proliv (Russian): strait
Punta (Spanish): point
Reservoir (English): *Res.*
Río (Spanish): river, *R.*
River (English): *R.*
Salto (Spanish, Portuguese): waterfall
Serra (Portuguese): mountain chain, *Sa.*
Shan (Chinese): mountains
Sierra (Spanish): mountain range, *Sa.*
Sound (English): *Sd.*
Vodokhranilishche (Russian): reservoir, *Vdkhr.*
Volcano (English): *Vol.*

SUMMIT
GLACIER
HORIZON
ICEBERG
CRATER
DORMANT VOLCANO
ARM
OCEAN
FJORD
POINT
ATOLL
TIMBER
BAY
STRAIT
ARCHIPELAGO
CHANNEL
TOWN
DELTA
PLAIN
REEF
SOUND
BLUFF
WAVES
CAPE
SPIT
KNOB
SEA
SANDBAR
GULF
KNOLL
SHOAL
INLET
BREAKERS
BEACH
PENINSULA
ISTHMUS
LAGOON
PASTURE
HEADLAND
RIVER
PRECIPICE
LEVEE
SHORE LINE
CITY AND SEAPORT
BREAKWATER
HARBOR
WHARF
DOCK
BRIDGE
ISLAND
RIVER MOUTH
CULTIVATED LAND
ESTUARY
PIER
DIKE
AIRPORT
ROAD
HIGHWAY
FIELD
MEADOW